FALLING STARS

Air Crashes that Filled Rock and Roll Heaven

FALLING STARS

Air Crashes that Filled Rock and Roll Heaven

Rich Everitt

HH
HARBOR
HOUSE

AUGUSTA

FALLING STARS
Air Crashes That Filled Rock and Roll Heaven
By Rich Everitt
A Harbor House Book/2004

For information address:
> HARBOR HOUSE
> 111 10TH STREET
> AUGUSTA, GEORGIA 30901

Library of Congress Cataloging-in-Publication Data
Everitt, Rich.
Falling stars : air crashes that filled rock and roll heaven / by Rich Everitt.
>   p. cm.
> Includes bibliographical references (p.   ) and index.
> ISBN 1-891799-04-5 (hardcover : alk. paper)
> 1. Musicians--Death. 2. Aircraft accident victims--United States.
I.
Title.
ML394.E84 2004
782.42166'092'2--dc22

                              2004015181

Printed in the United States of America
10 9 8 7 6 5 4 3 2 1

This one is for the girls:
Susan, Ellen and Kate

CONTENTS

IF THERE'S A ROCK AND ROLL HEAVEN:

THEY'VE GOTTA HAVE A HELL OF A BAND:

FOREWORD

FALLING STARS: AIR CRASHES THAT FILLED ROCK AND ROLL HEAVEN represents a marriage of two passions – aviation and music. In my childhood, the radio was filled with the music of The Beatles and bulletins of America's best test pilots being launched into space. To me they were equal heroes.

Later I, like most of my teenage friends, picked up a guitar intent on becoming the next Bob Dylan. My desire to learn to play Rock 'n Roll eventually supplanted my interest in aviation and led me directly to the music of Buddy Holly, who in the space of a couple of extraordinarily productive years, had set the musical course for my generation and those to follow.

Eventually, I discovered the music of the others in this book: Ricky Nelson, who outgrew (musically and personally) his early status as the original Teen Idol; Patsy Cline, whose voice remains to this day the gold standard for women singers of Country and Pop; Otis Redding, who brought Soul music to white, middle-class America; Jim Croce, who populated his songs of hope and heartbreak with his distinctive, Runyon-esque characters; John Denver, the bespectacled golden boy of Country and Pop who sang as passionately about the joys of life in mountains as he did the lonesome heartache of lost love; The Lynyrd Skynyrd Band, who defined "Southern Rock" with some of the best music ever to come from a Rock 'n Roll stage; and Stevie Ray Vaughan, who survived his personal demons to reclaim his position as "one of the best guitarists in the world."

Many years later, having abandoned my hope of becoming the next Dylan – but not, of course, the dream – I returned to my early life's other passion, aviation. I became a licensed pilot and shamelessly parlayed my job as a broadcast journalist into the most exciting flying adventures I could find, including flights with the Thunderbirds and Blue Angels; a demonstration flight of an F-4 Phantom jet; a backseat flight in a T-33; and a leisurely flight over the Appalachians at the yoke of a DC-3.

Then, during one of those adventures – a coast-to-coast flight in a small single engine Cessna – my mind wandered. There are endless hours available for mind-wandering on a coast-to-coast flight at 10,000 feet above the desert in a small, single-engine airplane. Mine went back to all the music I loved to listen to and how many of the musicians the world had lost doing exactly what I was doing right then – flying. I wondered exactly what did cause Ricky Nelson's plane to catch fire and why did Jim Croce's airplane hit the pine "trees lining the winding road?"

After I landed, I contacted the National Transportation Safety Board for answers, and I was astonished by what I learned.

The media (and, yes, I am a card-carrying member) had done a pathetic job of getting it right when reporting the facts of the crashes that took away our musical heroes. In our frenzy to get on the air with the "breaking news," we provided near wall-to-wall coverage of these tragedies – at least for the first 24-hour news cycle. Then we moved on to the next crisis du jour, leaving our viewers with the lasting impression that our initial authoritative speculation (and that's all we can have in the first few days after a crash) was the final word.

Turns out, it wasn't.

The NTSB investigators do a remarkably thorough job of figuring out why a plane crashes. It takes months, sometimes years. Long after the reporters and photographers have packed up their gear, the NTSB finishes analyzing the data and issues its findings. In the crashes written about in this book, very often what really happened had little resemblance to what we initially reported.

This book is by no means an exhaustive study of each of these crashes or of the musicians involved. Volumes could be – and in some cases, have been – written about each. Armed with the conclusions of the NTSB, I originally intended this book simply to set the record straight. I hoped to present, as we in television say, a "dramatic recreation based on real events."

But during the process, it became something more – an opportunity to revisit old friends who had provided the soundtrack for our lives, an opportunity to be reacquainted, not so much with the tragic deaths but the remarkable lives of these extraordinary people, each of whom – as Otis might have said – had so much to live for.

ACKNOWLEDGEMENTS

IN MANY WAYS, having my name on the front of this book is similar to having my name on the opening credits of the newscasts I've anchored the past 20 years – merely the emblem of much hard work done by others. First among equals deserving of special thanks is Susan Everitt, the best editor – and wife – on the planet.

Ted Lopatkiewicz at the NTSB went above and beyond the call of duty. So, too, did Bill Griggs of *50's Magazine* and aviator Mike Ramsey. Artimus Pyle, former drummer of the Lynyrd Skynyrd Band, provided invaluable insight in three areas: survivor, aviator and musician.

The encouragement and stories of Mary Muehleisen, Maury Muehleisen's sister, proved invaluable. The Web site she maintains – www.maurymuehleisen.com – is a continuing tribute to her brother and her forthcoming book on the lives of Jim Croce and Maury is sure to be a "must read" for all of Jim and Maury's fans.

I also wish to thank another musician, my friend, "the Godfather of Soul," James Brown, for his encouragement, support and background stories.

I owe Harbor House Publisher Randall Floyd a special debt of gratitude for his encouragement, wisdom and nerve.

My friends and colleagues, including Steve Clements, former executive producer of *Gary Collins Hour Magazine* and the new Mickey Mouse Club; Sherry Foster, editor of *Augusta Magazine*; General Perry Smith, author/CBS analyst; Meteorologist Jeff Rucker; Professor Marcia Della-Guistina; WRCB-TV News Director Bill Wallace; WGNO-TV News Director Bob Noonan; Editor/Photographer Greg Glass; and WDAM-TV General Manager Jim Cameron. Russell, Russ and Ronnie Everitt each provided inspiration, aid and comfort whether they know it or not.

And, most especially, I wish to thank Scott "Doogie" Myers, my research assistant, who did all the heavy lifting. Doogie not only made this book happen, he made it fun.

And, lastly I must thank my mentor, Trevanian, wherever he might be…

If There's a
Rock and Roll Heaven...

THAT'LL BE THE DAY...

Buddy Holly
Ritchie Valens
J.P. Richardson

Died: Feb. 3, 1959, Mason City, Iowa

THICK CLOUDS HANG LOW AND LEADEN over the snow-crusted field as he steps from the car and braces against the bitter Iowa morning. The lifting fog reveals a desolate plain, a season earlier lush with waving crops, now frozen and forbidding.

On the indistinct horizon behind him, between the frosted ground and slate sky, sits the farmhouse of Albert Juhl.

In the distance before him, a thin barbwire line is drawn across the open plain. He shuts the car door and crunches his way through the shallow snow. Step by heavy step, he makes his way toward an odd place at the distant fence — a strange, dark spot against the long straight line, like a period in the middle of a sentence. Laden with thick winter clothes, he struggles across the quiet plain until he comes upon a deep scar in the snow.

He follows it with growing urgency toward the strange ball piled against the fence. Strewn along the way he passes curious bits of metal, parts of an instrument panel and finally, a large piece of an airplane wing. Closer, he comes upon a man's shoe

1

and a small suitcase. He trudges the final steps to the wreckage and stops.

In the awful silence of the lonesome morning he surveys the sickening scene before him. A tangled ball of wreckage is heaped against the barbed wire fence, a person's gray, frozen legs protruding from it. The mangled body of a teenage boy lies face down in the bloody snow a few feet from the wreckage. A second body, clad in a ripped yellow jacket, much of his head missing, rests a few feet from the first. A third, larger body, prone and frozen, has been flung into the adjacent field beyond the fence.

He picks up a small pocket case and wipes off the snow to read the engraving on the side: "Ritchie Valens."

Alone on the barren plain, he is the only person who knows what minutes later will stun the world. Fine snow drifts lightly over the pallid bodies. It is the morning of Feb. 3, 1959 – the day the music died.

Buddy Holly

THE FIRST INKLING he had any musical talent came when Charles Hardin Holley, then 5 years old, and his brothers, Larry and Travis, sang *Down the River of Memories* at a local talent show. They won $5.

Music was part of the fabric and texture of the Holley household, apparently stemming from the maternal genes. Mother, Ella, had sung since childhood. Oldest brother Larry was a trained violinist. Brother Travis played the accordion and sister Pat played piano and sang. Father Lawrence's musical contribution was ... well, they say he was a very good listener.

Lawrence O'dell "L.O." Holley moved his family from Vernon, Texas, to Lubbock in 1925; the year his oldest son, Larry, was born. He was hoping for a better future and counting on Lubbock's economy to provide it. He supported his growing family – Travis was born in 1927, Patricia in 1929 – through the toughest days of the Depression by working a variety of jobs: short order cook, tailor and carpenter. L.O. and Ella's fourth and last child was born Sept. 7, 1936. They named him Charles Hardin, but quickly decided that was a mouthful. So, they called him "Buddy."

Buddy Holley followed in his siblings' musical footsteps. He studied violin, piano and steel guitar. Unlike his brothers and sister, his interest waned after a few years and wasn't rekindled until Travis returned from the U.S. Marine Corps with a cheap guitar from a pawnshop. He showed Buddy a few chords and, before long, Buddy was the teacher and Travis the student.

By the time Buddy began classes at J.T. Hutchinson Junior High School in 1949 he was already a "triple threat" – a whiz on the guitar, banjo and mandolin. He and his friend, fellow 13-year-old classmate Bob Montgomery, soaked up the influences they heard on the radio: Hank Williams, Bill Monroe, Jim and Jesse, the Louisiana Hayride and, of course, the Grand Ole Opry.

With an ever-changing succession of local musicians joining them, Buddy and Bob spent their junior high and high school years playing anywhere they could find an audience. One former band member later recalled, "We'd play for the opening of a pack of cigarettes."

By their late teens, Buddy and Bob had become popular musicians in the Lubbock area, playing music they called "Western Bop." They had their own program, *The Buddy and Bob Show*, on KDAV radio and they were opening regularly for major Country music stars at area clubs and the local coliseum. The career in Country music of which Buddy had dreamed seemed to be taking shape.

That's when Elvis came to town.

The world was quickly becoming familiar with Elvis, and Buddy and Bob were no exception. They were already fans, having heard on the radio *That's Alright* and *Good Rockin' Tonight*, two hits from Elvis' early Sun Records days. However, hearing Elvis was not the same as seeing him in person. Buddy got the opportunity when he opened the show for Elvis in Lubbock on Oct. 15, 1955.

Sonny Curtis, a "Buddy and Bob" band member, later told a writer for The Buddy Holly Center in Lubbock, "Presley just blew Buddy away. None of us had ever seen anything like Elvis, the way he could get the girls jumping up and down, and that definitely impressed Holly. But it was the music that really turned Buddy around. He loved Presley's rhythm ... it wasn't Country and it wasn't Blues ... it was somewhere in the middle. After seeing Elvis, Buddy had only one way to go."

In an interview with *Billboard Magazine*, Buddy spoke of Elvis as a musical Moses, leading an entire generation to the Rock 'n Roll Promised Land. "Without Elvis Presley," he said, "none of us would have made it."

However, Buddy's shift toward Rock 'n Roll might have cost him his first shot at musical stardom. In October 1955, Buddy and Bob opened for Bill Haley and the Comets at the Fair Park Coliseum. Singer Marty Robbins' manager, Eddie Crandall, was in the audience and liked what he saw. Since he also doubled as a talent agent, Crandall arranged a deal for Buddy (but not Bob) to record for Decca Records. Decca assigned legendary Country music producer Owen Bradley to oversee the sessions.

Bradley brought in Nashville studio musicians and produced two singles, *Blue Days, Black Nights/Love Me* and *Modern Don Juan/You Are My One Desire* with a formulaic Country approach. Neither record generated much interest.

"We had been very successful with a Country format; we were all into Country, and it's hard to change patterns. Buddy couldn't quite fit into our formula any more than we could fit into his ... he was unique, and he wasn't in a pattern. We didn't understand that, and he didn't know how to tell us," Bradley later told The Buddy Holly Center.

Decca did not renew Buddy's contract, but kept a number of unreleased cuts from the Nashville sessions including *Rock Around with Ollie Vee, Ting-A-Ling, Baby Won't You Come Out Tonight* and *That'll Be the Day*.

Buddy returned to Texas, happy to be back recording with his friends.

He spent the next few months with drummer/friend Jerry Allison cutting demos at studios throughout the Lubbock area.

They grew particularly fond of one owned by Norman Petty in Clovis, N.M., about 100 miles northwest of Lubbock. Petty had built the studio two years earlier to record his own trio and to make demos for other musicians. In addition to being a talented musician, he was an engineer and had rigged his studio with the best gear money could buy.

In the early morning of Feb. 25, 1957, Buddy, Jerry Allison, Larry Welborn, and Niki Sullivan gathered at Petty's studio for the recording session of unknown musician, Gary Tollett. Gary's wife, Ramona, was also present. The session lasted until the wee hours.

When they were done with Gary's songs, they recorded Buddy's *Lookin' for Someone to Love,* and the song he had built around John Wayne's often quoted line from the motion picture

The Searchers, That'll Be the Day.

The tapes of the session began winding their way through the music industry. At Roulette Records executives liked the songs but wanted a couple of their current artists – not Buddy – to record them. Buddy refused and sent the tapes to New York publishing house Peer-Southern. Peer-Southern sent the tapes to Brunswick Records, a subsidiary of Decca. Executives there liked the tape of *That'll Be the Day* so much they didn't bother to have Buddy re-cut it. They mastered the demo tape for release as a single.

But there was a legal problem. Buddy was forbidden to release any songs he recorded under his previous contract with Decca and one of those songs was, *That'll be the Day*. Therefore, he would have to release the new version of *That'll Be the Day* under a different name. Buddy and Jerry Allison thumbed through a dictionary searching for one. Initially they decided on "The Beetles," but changed their mind agreeing that "The Crickets" had a nicer ring to it.

"Buddy Holly" and "The Crickets" might seem synonymous, but legally they were quite distinct. There were actually two recording contracts for Buddy. The first, with Brunswick, was for songs released by The Crickets with whom Buddy performed. The second was with Coral Records, another Decca subsidiary, for records released as a solo artist under Buddy's own name, which was misspelled as Holly.

Brunswick released The Crickets' version of *That'll Be the Day* in summer 1957 and it exploded onto the charts. With a recording contract and a hit record, all The Crickets needed now was a good manager to guide their blooming career. They hired their friend Norman Petty.

With his "hiccup" vocals, added syllables and open chord guitar strumming, Buddy was a radio hit. However, it was not simply Buddy's unusual vocal styling and guitar playing that gave The Crickets their unique sound. It was Buddy's prowess in the recording studio, too.

In those days, before large multi-track recording studios, most bands recorded "live-to-tape" – they would simply turn on a tape recorder and play the song over and over until they got it right. Buddy had a better idea: Why not use two tape recorders? Record the basic track – drums, guitar, bass and vocals on one, then play it back while the second recorder tapes it, plus any additional music being played by the musicians live. "Double tracking" allowed Buddy to sing harmony with himself and play lead guitar licks on top of his own rhythm guitar.

Compared to today's digital studios with their endless number of tracks and effects, double tracking seems downright crude, but in its day it was a clever innovation. And it gave Buddy Holly a unique sound.

During summer 1957, that sound seemed to jump from every transistor at the beach and dashboard on the strip. Across America, teens suddenly discovered Buddy Holly and The Crickets on the radio. Now they wanted to see them in person.

In fall 1957, Buddy and The Crickets – now solidified as Jerry Allison on drums, Joe Mauldin on bass and Niki Sullivan on rhythm guitar – joined the Everly Brothers and Fats Domino on an 80-city tour. Along the way, Petty booked them into a studio in Oklahoma City where they recorded songs for their first album, *The Chirping Crickets*. Among other songs recorded during those session were the rock classics *Oh Boy*, which Buddy had originally titled *All My Love*, and *Peggy Sue*, which he'd originally titled *Cindy Lou* (for his niece) but changed in honor of Allison's girlfriend, Peggy Sue Gerron.

Coral released *Peggy Sue* as the first record under Buddy's name as a solo artist while Brunswick released *Oh Boy* under The Crickets' name. By December 1957, both songs were roaring up the charts. Suddenly Buddy's record sales rivaled those of his idol, Elvis Presley.

Even with their radio success, record sales and tour, most of America still had not actually seen Buddy Holly and The Crickets. Many mistakenly thought they were a black act. The confusion led Buddy and The Crickets to become the first white band to play the legendary Apollo Theater in Harlem.

Initially, the audience gave Buddy and The Crickets a cold reception but finally warmed to the white boys in white shirts when Holly opened the third show with a Bo Diddley number. A quick succession of TV appearances on *American Bandstand*, the *Arthur Murray Dance Party* and the *Ed Sullivan Show* resolved the identity crisis.

American teens were not the only ones suddenly raving about Buddy Holly and The Crickets. They were selling millions of records overseas, too. In February 1958, they joined a wildly popular tour of Australia with Paul Anka and Jerry Lee Lewis. In March, they followed the Australian tour with an equally successful 25-day tour of England that led *Melody Maker* magazine to gush, "Country fans need look no further than *Peggy Sue* and Buddy Holly is every bit as good as on the disc."

The importance of the tour of England is difficult to overstate. It changed the course of popular music by giving the founding fathers of what was to become the "British Invasion" an inspiring look at American Rock 'n Roll. From John Lennon and Paul McCartney to Keith Richards and Mick Jagger, British musicians saw their future in the music of Buddy Holly.

Buddy and The Crickets returned to the United States and continued their relentless touring while the record company continued releasing their records. By then, Buddy and The Crickets were hitting the charts with astonishing rapidity: *That'll be the Day, Peggy Sue, Listen to Me, Maybe Baby, Oh Boy, Think it Over, Rave On.* There seemed no end to Buddy's Midas Touch.

Buddy Holly and The Crickets was the hottest band on tour ,but that was not enough to sustain Crickets guitarist Niki Sullivan. He had grown weary of the road and left the band. Buddy asked Tommy Allsup to fill in. Initially, Allsup's role was restricted to the studio, but by summer 1958, he was touring with the band as well. That summer another person also entered Buddy's life: Maria Elena Santiago.

In June 1958, Buddy paid a visit to his publisher's office, Peer-Southern Organization, in New York City. There he met Maria, the receptionist. By all accounts, it was love at first sight and Buddy asked Maria to marry him on their first or second (depending on who is telling the story) date.

Two months later, Aug. 15, 1958, the Holley family gathered in their Lubbock home for Buddy's Baptist minister to perform the ceremony. On that day, Buddy tied the knot with Maria and cut his ties with Lubbock. After a honeymoon in Acapulco, he and Maria moved into an apartment near New York City's Greenwich Village.

Living in New York kept Buddy closer to the center of the music business, but it kept him further from The Crickets and his manager, Norman Petty. As he became savvier in the "business" of the music business, Buddy became less willing for Petty to manage his affairs. It strained their relationship and, as summer turned to fall, the association between Buddy and Petty worsened. Finally, it reached crisis proportions in October, after the last tour of 1958.

At a meeting between Buddy, Petty, Allison and Maudlin in

Lubbock on Nov. 3, 1958, the division between them was simple and stark. Allison and Maudlin wanted to continue with Petty as their manager. Buddy did not. He ended his relationship with both Petty and The Crickets that day, but with the understanding he would welcome The Crickets back if they ever changed their minds. And that was that. Buddy returned to Maria in New York to figure out what to do next.

He spent the rest of 1958 burning his energies in a burst of creativity. He wrote and recorded new songs, made plans for another tour and helped promote the careers of several unknown artists, among them an old friend from Texas, bass player/disc jockey Waylon Jennings.

Still, his most productive act as 1958 ended was not professional, but personal. Maria became pregnant with their first child. Consequently, she decided not to join Buddy in late January for his first tour of the New Year – an ill conceived, three-week swing through the mid-west billed as "The Winter Dance Party" tour.

Without The Crickets to back him, Buddy recruited new musicians for the tour: guitarist Tommy Allsup, the "unofficial" Cricket who had replaced Niki Sullivan, drummer Carl Bunch and bassist Waylon Jennings. Although they were not The Crickets, some promoters misled audiences by continuing to promote them as The Crickets.

It was a "package" tour that included several other acts on the bill: Dion and the Belmonts; unknown singer Frankie Sardo; a 28-year-old disc jockey from Beaumont, Texas, named J.P. Richardson, better known as "The Big Bopper;" and 17-year-old Californian sensation Ritchie Valens, whose record *Donna* was the hottest song on the radio.

Ritchie Valens

RITCHIE VALENS WAS THE FIRST Hispanic Rock 'n Roll star, but his influence exceeded demographics.

Richard Steven Valenzuela was the second of five children born to his impoverished Pacoima, California family. His father, Joseph Steven Valenzuela, raised Ritchie after his parents divorce, struggling to earn a living as a tree surgeon, horse trainer and munitions plant worker. When he died of complications from diabetes, Ritchie, 10, moved in with his mother, Concepcion, and three siblings. He was regularly shuttled off to live with his aunts and uncles and from them he learned an appreciation for Mexican music. Quickly, that appreciation became a passion.

Although an average student in the classroom, Ritchie excelled at entertaining his fellow students at Pacoima Junior High School during lunch breaks or assembly programs.

In his junior year at San Fernando High School, he joined The Silhouettes Rock 'n Roll band. They became popular locally and the buzz attracted the attention of Bob Keane, president of Keane Records.

Keane Records was enjoying phenomenal success with a string of hits by Sam Cooke, and Bob was hoping to find another young talent for his newly formed Del-Fi Records. In May 1958, he summoned Ritchie to Los Angeles for an audition. With tape rolling, Ritchie played an instrumental with lyrics he added on the spot. The audition needed no improvement, but Richard Valenzuela's name did. Keane released the audition tape as the single *Come On, Let's Go* by Ritchie Valens in summer 1958. By August, it was a national hit. Keane had found his new young star.

Keane sent Ritchie out on a short tour to capitalize on the

popularity of *Come On, Let's Go*. But Keane also wanted new records, so in October he brought Ritchie back into the studio to cut two more songs to be released as a single "double-sided" 45-rpm record. The A side was a ballad Ritchie had written for his high school girlfriend, Donna Ludwig.

Donna was a dreamy ode-to-love about which singer Billy Vera later wrote, "Slow dancing to it, you and your baby could get lost in virtual layers of romance."

The more teens slow danced to it, the faster it climbed the charts, astonishingly to No. 2 on the Pop charts and No. 11 on the R & B charts. Then something even more astonishing happened. They flipped the record over and discovered the timeless classic, *La Bamba*. The Mexican folk tune, given a Rock 'n Roll beat by Ritchie, sent teens in America into a sock-hoppin' frenzy, even though most never realized the Spanish lyrics urged them to do it with grace. It sold one million copies.

The three back-to-back hits made Ritchie the hottest new act in music, so in January 1959, Keane booked him on the biggest tour of the season, The Winter Dance Party.

J.P. Richardson, The Big Bopper

ALSO, ON THE TOUR was a Rock 'n Roll novelty known as The Big Bopper. The Bopper was, in reality, Jiles Perry "J.P." Richardson, a Texas disc jockey and aspiring Pop star and songwriter. He had signed with Mercury Records in 1957 and although his first two songs, *Beggar to a King* and *Crazy Blues*, fell flat, the third song was the charm. *Chantilly Lace* became radio's third most frequently played song of 1958. He followed that with *Purple People*

Eater Meets the Witch Doctor, Little Red Riding Hood and *The Big Bopper's Wedding.*

While Richardson was a husband with a son and a daughter, his alter ego, The Big Bopper, with his checkered zoot suits and booming baritone, was a larger-than-life presence on stage and a consummate showman. He frequently toured to promote his records and his addition to the Winter Dance Party was sure to provide its share of comic relief.

THERE WAS NOTHING FUNNY about the miserable traveling conditions of the tour, which began in Milwaukee, Wisconsin, on Jan. 23, 1959. Buddy, Ritchie, the Bopper and the others spent the next week in a freezing bus crisscrossing the snowy highways of the midwest for a string of one-night stands in Kenosha, Mankato, Eau Claire, Monteviedeo, St. Paul, Davenport, Fort Dodge and Duluth.

Finally, the bus, its heater broken, gave up the ghost on the road near Appleton, Wis. As the temperature dropped to 30 degrees below zero, the passengers burned newspapers in the aisle. By the time help arrived, Buddy's drummer, Carl Bunch, was suffering from frostbite. The show in Appleton was cancelled, but their wretched situation became worse as flu spread among the performers and the only replacement bus they could find was an old school bus.

Still, they pressed on to Green Bay, Wis., for a show at the Riverside Ballroom.

By the next afternoon, Feb. 2, as the tour limped toward Clear Lake, Iowa, Buddy had enough of freezing buses and decided to do something about it – he would rent an airplane to take him to the next stop in Moorhead, Minn. In addition to getting him out of the cold, it would save enough time to get some rest and maybe even do some laundry.

The nearest airport is in Mason City, Iowa. It is operated by The Dwyer Flying Service. Hubert Dwyer started his company six years earlier and provides just about any service an airport might need: student instruction, aircraft sales, maintenance and charter flights.

The manager of the Surf Ballroom, Carroll Anderson, calls Dwyer with some exciting news. One of the hottest Rock 'n Roll acts in the world would like to charter one of Dwyer's airplane's for a flight to Fargo, N.D., after their performance. Dwyer says he will have a pilot and plane for Buddy, and band members Tommy and Waylon, ready after the show.

It does not take long for word to get around among the performers that Holly has chartered an airplane. After a week freezing on buses, an airplane flight is irresistible, so the angling for a seat begins. Since it is Buddy's charter, no one tries to talk him out of his seat. Tommy and Waylon, however, are fair game.

Ritchie bugs Tommy throughout the evening. Ritchie figures it is only fair that he should get a seat on the plane. After all, Tommy has flown on airplanes. Ritchie never has. Finally, Tommy flips a coin and Ritchie calls "Heads." Heads it is. Tommy is off the flight and Ritchie is on.

Next, The Bopper approaches Waylon and explains he is tired and sick with the flu and, because he is so large, he can't sleep or even rest comfortably in the cramped bus, but if he could fly to the next stop he could rest and maybe get well. Could he have Waylon's seat on the plane?

Without much thought or discussion, Waylon agrees and The Bopper has his coveted spot on the plane too.

Years later, Waylon described for his biographer a discussion with Buddy later that night.

"He had me go get us some hotdogs. He was leaning back

against the wall in a cane-bottom chair and he was laughing at me. He said, 'So, you're not going with us tonight on the plane, huh? Well, I hope your ol' bus freezes up. It's 40 below out there and you're gonna get awful cold.'

"So, I said, 'Well, I hope your ol' plane crashes.'"

THE SHOW FINISHES BEFORE MIDNIGHT and Buddy, Ritchie and The Bopper leave the concert hall's cheering fans to join Carroll Anderson, his wife and 8-year-old son for a ride to the airport in the family car.

Pilot Roger Peterson, 21, has spent the day preparing for the flight. Dwyer hired him about a year earlier as a commercial pilot and flight instructor. On this night, he will be flying the most important people he has ever flown. For a young, newly married man trying to build a life around flying, this is a big flight, especially for someone with such modest experience and training.

Peterson has been flying since 1954 and has accumulated just over 700 hours of flight time. He has taken 52 hours of instrument flight training and passed his written instrument flight exam. However, he failed his instrument check ride nine months earlier and, consequently, is restricted from flying in weather conditions that require the use of instruments to fly safely.

He stops by the air traffic communications station in the airport's tower at 5:17 p.m. to get his first weather briefing. Visibilities throughout the area are 10 miles or better, and ceilings are 5,000 feet or better. There might be a little snow moving into the Fargo area around 2 a.m., and a cold front is expected to pass Fargo at 4 a.m. Not perfect weather, but nothing scary either.

By the time he calls for an update at 11:20 p.m., the weather has deteriorated slightly. Now the stations along his route are reporting ceilings of 4,200 feet or better. Still, visibilities are 10 miles or better but the cold front is now expected to pass Fargo at 2 a.m. instead of the previously forecast 4 a.m. The weather in Mason City is the best in the area: ceilings 6,000 feet; visibility better than 15 miles, but it's bitterly cold – 15 degrees, and the wind is howling at nearly 29 miles per hour with gusts up to almost 37 miles per hour.

At 11:55 p.m. Dwyer personally accompanies Peterson to the weather office to check the latest weather information. Locally, it has deteriorated even more. The ceiling has dropped down to 5,000, light snow is falling, and the pressure has fallen from 29.96 to 29.90.

At 12:40 a.m., Anderson's car pulls up with his family and celebrity passengers. They gather a large brown leather suitcase and several smaller travel bags from the car and hurry toward the airplane where Peterson and Dwyer are waiting. After the passengers and bags are loaded, Peterson tells Dwyer he will file his flight plan by radio once the airplane is in the air.

The airplane is a 12-year-old Beech Bonanza with the tail number N3794N. The Bonanza was the first high performance airplane introduced after World War II. Considered the Mercedes of airplanes by many pilots, it enjoys a reputation befitting its slick design and stellar performance. A low-wing airplane, its most noticeable feature is its tail. Unlike most air-planes, which have both a vertical and horizontal stabilizer for tail feathers, the Bonanza has only two wings at the rear, mount-ed in a V-tail configuration. With its slippery design and 185 horses under the cowl, a 1947 Bonanza can climb at about 1,000 feet per minute and cruise at about 167 miles per hour.

Within the cabin, passengers enjoy plush creature comforts akin to a luxury automobile, although front seat passengers might enjoy the ride more than those in the rear. According to

Aviation Consumer, "Rear passengers in V-tail Bonanzas are usually miserable in turbulence … the V-tail looks neat and is the shining symbol of the Bonanza line, but it does a lousy job as a tail. In turbulence, the V-tail models fishtail excessively, usually requiring several oscillations to recover from a good jolt."

The turbulence will be considerable tonight. As Peterson taxis the Bonanza to the end of runway 17, the airplane is buffeted by winds exceeding 20 miles per hour with gusts over 30 miles per hour. At altitude it will be worse. He radios the weather station and learns the weather along his intended route has not changed much, but the local weather has. The ceiling has dropped to 3,000 feet, light snow is falling, visibilities are down to six miles and the pressure is continuing to drop.

Dwyer and the Anderson family watch the lights of the Bonanza accelerate down the darkened runway and lift into the air. The airplane climbs to 800 feet and makes a 180-degree turn, passing the airport to the east to head in a northwesterly direction. From a platform outside the tower, Dwyer watches the airplane fly off into the darkness, the tail light gradually descending until out of sight. He goes to the office to make sure Peterson has checked in by radio to file his flight plan and is surprised to learn the radio operator has not heard from him.

Carroll Anderson and his family climb back into their car and head home. It is not every night you give a lift to the biggest entertainers in world. This will be a night to remember.

At Dwyer's request, the radio operator tries to raise Peterson. No answer. He tries again and again. For the next several minutes, Dwyer and the operator hover over the radio calling and listening. There is no response. Something is wrong.

Peterson is struggling with the Bonanza. The darkness and snow make it impossible to get his bearings by looking out the window. He focuses on the airplane's "attitude indicator"– a mechanical instrument that visually represents the earth and the airplane's attitude in the sky – but it makes no sense. He does not know if he is climbing or descending. He is unsure if the plane is banking left or right. He looks out the window to orient himself, but there are no ground lights, no stars – just a black void.

Suddenly, the right wingtip slams into the ground and sends the airplane cartwheeling – breaking and slinging parts and people over the course of 570 feet of tumbling, grinding violence. As the wreckage skids across the stubble field, it breaks and bends into an unrecognizable mass of torn and tangled metal finally sliding to rest against a barbwire fence. A light snow falls as quiet descends once again on the desolate plain.

In Clear Lake, teens are still buzzing about the Winter Dance Party Show at the Surf Ballroom. The excitement lingers until the wee hours on telephone lines and at gathering places, while a few miles away the bodies of a young pilot and the hottest rock stars in the world lie cooling in the darkness on a lonesome plain.

BY DAYBREAK, there has been no word from Peterson and Dwyer is sick with worry. As soon as the weather clears, he takes off to search for the Bonanza by air. He has barely begun his climb when he spots something in a snowy field a few miles ahead. He radios in the report and the local sheriff's office dispatches Deputy Bill McGill to the site.

McGill steps out of his patrol car and into the frigid Iowa morning. Near the horizon behind him is the farmhouse of Albert Juhl. Facing him is a snowy expanse split by a thin barbwire fence, a strange rubble piled against it. He hikes over to it, surveys the carnage and finds a pocket case engraved with the name, "Ritchie Valens." He calls in his report and a short time later, before the bodies are moved, the field is crawling with deputies, highway patrolmen, reporters, photographers and spectators.

They send out the bulletin to a stunned world: Buddy Holly, Ritchie Valens and The Big Bopper are dead.

THE CIVIL AERONAUTICS BOARD, the predecessor to NTSB, placed most of the blame on pilot Peterson, but tarred others with the same brush.

First, the CAB noted that despite multiple requests for weather information, the weather communicators on duty only provided Peterson with current conditions along his intended route and the forecast for his destination. They apparently failed to provide Peterson with two critical "Flash" advisories issued that night by the National Weather Service. Both were issued before the flight took off – the first at 11:35 p.m. and the second at 12:15 a.m. Both advisories predicted much worse weather than the information Peterson had been given, including "*locally heavy icing ... freezing drizzle*." The flashes also contained dire predictions of low ceilings, low visibilities and strong gusty winds.

According to the CAB, "*Failure of the communicators to draw these advisories to the attention of the pilot and to emphasize their importance could readily lead the pilot to underestimate the severity of the weather situation.*" But also, "*the pilot and operator (Dwyer) in this case had a definite responsibility to request and obtain all of the available information and to interpret it correctly. At Mason City, at the time of takeoff, the barometer was falling, the ceiling and visibility were lowering, light snow had begun to fall, and the surface winds and winds aloft were so high one could reasonably have expected to encounter adverse weather during the estimated two hour flight.*"

Considering the weather conditions and "*the pilot's unproven ability to fly by instrument, the decision to go seems most imprudent.*"

In short, according to the CAB, Peterson should have cancelled the flight because weather conditions exceeded his abilities. Did he simply not realize, as the CAB suggests, that the weather was so bad? Even though he was never provided the Flash advisories, the forecasts he had received throughout the day showed a worsening trend. Or did he believe his skills as a pilot were sufficient for the circumstance? Or was it simply emotionally impossible for a 21-year-old pilot to say "No" to three Rock heroes? Whatever the reason, Peterson did not cancel the flight and the trouble began almost immediately.

"*It is believed that shortly after takeoff pilot Peterson entered an area of complete darkness and one in which there was no definite horizon; that the snow conditions and the lack of horizon required him to rely solely on flight instruments for aircraft attitude and orientation. The high gusty winds and the attendant turbulence which existed would have caused*"...most of the instruments to fluctuate so wildly as to be unreliable ... "*With his limited experience the pilot would tend to rely on the attitude gyro which is relatively stable under these conditions,*" the CAB reported.

Reliance on the attitude gyro would have presented twin dilemmas for Peterson. First, he was not qualified to fly by sole reference to his instruments. Although he had taken hours of instrument flying instruction, he had flunked his instrument flight test nine months earlier. Second, the display on the Bonanza's attitude gyro was opposite from the one with which Peterson had trained.

"*Therefore, he could have become confused and thought that he was making a climbing turn when in reality he was making a descending turn,*" the CAB concluded.

The CAB concluded the crash was Peterson's fault for *"his unwise decision to embark on a flight which would necessitate flying solely by instruments when he was not properly certificated or qualified to do so. Contributing factors were serious deficiencies in the weather briefing, and the pilot's unfamiliarity with the instrument which determines the attitude of the aircraft."*

LATER IN THE MORNING, Carroll Anderson, who had driven the performers from the Surf Ballroom to the airport, arrived at the crash site and identified the bodies. Deputy McGill helped open the wreckage with metal cutting tools to remove Peterson's body.

That afternoon Buddy's latest record, *It Doesn't Matter*, entered the Top 100. On the flipside, fans discovered a song which expressed the feelings of an entire generation that day – *Raining in My Heart*.

PETERSON WAS LAID TO REST Feb. 6 in his hometown of Alta, Iowa.

The body of J.P. Richardson was flown home to Texas in a private airplane and interred in the Beaumont Cemetery on Feb. 5, 1959. Elvis and Colonel Tom Parker sent yellow roses.

Richard Steven Valenzuela's body was sent by train back to San Fernando Valley. At the age of 17, he had shaken the world of music with only three songs: *Come on Let's Go, Donna* and *La Bamba*. His family laid him to rest in the San Fernando Valley Cemetery and inscribed on his tombstone: "Come On, Let's Go." He was inducted into the Rock and Roll Hall of Fame in 2001.

A service for Buddy Holly was held Feb. 7, 1959, at the Tabernacle Baptist Church in Lubbock. More than 1,000 mourners attended.

Other performers have had more hits, but few have had the impact of Buddy. He had said that Elvis led his generation into

Rock 'n Roll, and just as surely, Buddy led the next. By inspiring performers from The Beatles to Bob Dylan, Buddy changed the course of popular music, and he did it in less than two years.

He was inducted into the Rock and Roll Hall of Fame in 1986. His widow, Maria, accepted the honor on his behalf. Perhaps Buddy was right when, as a teenager in Lubbock, he had told Jerry Allison's girlfriend, "It's destiny, Peggy Sue...everything is destiny."

THE WINTER DANCE PARTY TOUR soldiered on without Buddy, Ritchie and the Big Bopper. The promoter pressed Fabian and Frankie Avalon into service as substitute headliners and hired an unknown high school sophomore from Fargo to fill in for the show in Moorhead, Minn.

In doing so, he unwittingly launched the career of 1960s sensation Bobby Vee.

Dion DiMucci continues to enjoy a career in popular music.

Waylon Jennings became a legend of Country music.

The original Crickets remain a popular attraction at Oldies shows.

After his debut in Moorhead, Bobby Vee expanded his band to include a piano player – a "wiry kid" from Hibbing, Minn., named Bobby Zimmerman who did OK, too. Eventually, he changed his last name to "Dylan."

Oddities and Ironies

J.P. RICHARDSON WROTE George Jones' first country hit, *White Lightning* and Johnny Preston's hit, *Running Bear*.

Before becoming a Pop star, The Big Bopper's claim to fame

was achieved as a Texas disc jockey. He once set a record for broadcasting continuously for more than five straight days, spinning more than 1,800 records.

Waylon Jennings and Tommy Allsup are not the only ones who did not get on the ill-fated airplane. Dion DiMucci turned down Buddy's offer to let him take the flight because it was going to cost $36 per person, a ridiculously high price in Dion's view.

A recording by Mick Jagger and Keith Richards of *La Bamba* – made in a friend's living room when they were teenagers – later sold for more than $80,000.00.

The editor of *Rockin' 50's* music magazine, Bill Griggs, claims that J.P. Richardson, not Ricky Nelson, made the first music video when he filmed *Chantilly Lace* in 1958 and, furthermore, coined the term "music video."

Buddy's wife, Maria, was pregnant with their first child at the time of the crash. She later lost the baby.

The airplane was never named "American Pie," "Miss American Pie," or any other kind of pie. It was simply registered as N3794N.

Waylon Jennings named his son after Buddy.

Tommy, who lost his seat on the plane when Ritchie called "Heads," later owned a restaurant called, "Heads Up."

The Rolling Stones first hit was a cover of Buddy's *Not Fade Away*.

In January 1956, Buddy performed on a short "package tour" with Cowboy Copas. Four years after Buddy's crash, Copas would die in an airplane crash with Patsy Cline.

...AND THEN GOODBYE

Patsy Cline
Hawkshaw Hawkins
Cowboy Copas

Died: March 5, 1963, Camden, Tenn.

Pasty Cline

IN AN INSTANT OF VIOLENCE her face slams through the glass, a jagged edge slicing a deep gash across her forehead. The impact breaks her ribs and wrist, and rips her hip from its socket. Inertia tears her organs from their internal moorings and flings her through the windshield like an angrily tossed Raggedy Ann. The collision goes on and on – crashing glass, grinding metal, bending and breaking steel, a smear of color, and a cacophony of noise.

Finally, the ill-tuned orchestra of screeching discordant notes goes quiet except for some last bits of metal falling to a clanking finale on the asphalt, and the hissing of steam spewing from the cracked motor. She lies motionless and broken amid a twisted tableau of smoking steel, shattered glass, and dripping blood – the aftermath of a grinding car crash outside a Nashville high school.

This accident was her second brush with death. Years earlier, she had survived rheumatic fever. It began with a sore throat and ended with doctors resuscitating her after her heart stopped beating. She spent days in an oxygen tent and eventually recovered with only a single lasting effect – the infection of her throat had miraculously changed her voice into a "booming voice like Kate Smith's."

Just as her first brush with death blessed her with a magnificent voice, her second – the horrific automobile accident in front of Madison High School on June 14, 1961 – gifted her as well. During the month she spent in a Nashville hospital bed, the publicity surrounding the accident helped push Patsy Cline's newly recorded song, *I Fall to Pieces*, up the Country music charts to become her first No. 1 Country hit.

Two years after the accident, she recalled both near misses when leaving the Ryman Auditorium. Ray Walker, a member of the Jordanaires, cautioned Patsy to be careful flying to an upcoming concert.

"Honey," she told him, "I've been in two bad ones ... the third one will either be the charm, or it'll kill me."

THE WOMAN WITH THE BIG VOICE was born in the small town of Gore near Winchester, W. Va., on Sept. 8, 1932, six days after her 16-year-old mother married her much older father.

Sam and Hilda Hensley named her Virginia Patterson Hensley and called her Ginnie. She was the third mouth the impoverished parents would have to feed. Sam already had two children from a previous marriage. It was a peripatetic life. Her blacksmith father moved the family almost constantly – more than 20 times – until finally settling in Winchester in Ginnie's eighth-grade year.

During those early years, Ginnie's artistic bent was toward dancing. She had seen Shirley Temple in a movie and decided she wanted to dance. She became good enough to win first place in a local talent competition, but eventually her love of song supplanted her desire to tap. Her financially strapped parents scraped up the money to buy a piano for her eighth birthday, but not the lessons that went with it. So Ginnie taught herself, and by her early teens, she was playing piano and singing in church.

Her middle teens were difficult. Sam abandoned the family when Ginnie was 15, and by the age of 16, she was forced quit John Handley High School to work a variety of odd jobs to help support her mother and two half siblings.

She worked in the kitchen at Gus Kanis' Capital Restaurant (where her mother was a waitress); as a waitress at the Red Wing Restaurant and at the Greyhound Bus food counter; and as a soda fountain clerk at Gaunt's Drug Store. At night, she sang anywhere she could – talent shows, taverns and dances, and she became a regular performer on WINC radio in Winchester.

In 1952, at the age of 20, Ginnie became the singer for The Melody Boys, a regional Country band led by disc jockey and erstwhile salesman Bill Peer. Peer suggested Ginnie change her name to Patsy, a tortured contraction of her middle name, Patterson.

A few months later in February 1953, after a courtship of only a few weeks, Patsy married Gerald Cline. The night of their wedding, she appeared on stage for the first time as "Patsy Cline." The marriage was unhappy and brief, but the name stuck.

Peer, acting as Patsy's manager, shopped her demo tape around Nashville and arranged a deal with William McColl, president of Four Star Records. A small label once owned by Gene Autry, its only major act was Jimmy Dean.

It was not the "Big Time" of which she had dreamed, but it was a bona fide recording contract – unfortunately, one rife with the worst of fine print. By signing it, Patsy gave away her artistic rights. She could only record the songs McColl selected, and he selected only songs to which he held publishing rights. This assured him of receiving not only label royalties, but publishing royalties too – a classic case of double dipping. Next, McColl worked a deal to lease Patsy's recordings to Decca Records. It was a good deal for McColl and a horrible deal for Patsy, but at least it was a deal, and that was more than she had ever had.

In summer 1955, Patsy went into the recording studio for her first session under her Four Star contract. She recorded four songs: *A Church, a Courtroom then Good-bye; Turn the Card Slowly; Honky-tonk Merry Go Round* and *Hiding Out.* None of the songs made the charts, and Patsy was sent back into the studio in winter and spring 1956 to try again. This time McColl picked the up-tempo tunes, *I Love You Honey* and *Stop, Look and Listen.*

These were failures, too.

Songwriter Don Hecht suggested Patsy record a bluesy song he had written for Kay Starr, which Starr had rejected. The straight-talking Patsy wanted to reject it too, calling it "nothing but a little ol' pop song." However, because she had signed away her artistic rights, she was compelled to record it. So, in November 1956, Patsy returned to the studio and recorded three more songs: *A Poor Man's Roses, The Heart You Break May Be Your Own*, and that "little ol' pop song" – *Walking After Midnight.*

The following January, Patsy sang *Walking After Midnight* on the nationally broadcast *Arthur Godfrey's Talent Scouts Show.* When Decca released it as a single two weeks later, it shot to the top of the Country charts. Then it did something that astonished everyone – it jumped to the top of the Pop charts, too.

When Decca released the "B" side, *A Poor Man's Roses*, it became an instant hit as well. Suddenly, Patsy Cline had become one of the first "cross-over" artists in Country music history. What happened next was almost as improbable: The hits stopped as suddenly as they had begun.

Patsy returned to the studio in spring 1957 to record 14 songs that were to be her debut album. It was released in early August 1957, but failed to produce a single hit song. Still, on the strength of *Walking after Midnight* and *A Poor Man's Roses*, *Billboard Magazine* named Patsy the Most Promising Country and Western Female Artist of 1957.

"Promising" more hits, but where were they?

Patsy's personal life was suffering swings as wild as her professional one.

Her stormy marriage to Gerald Cline officially ended, and she married "the love of (her) life," Charlie Dick, whom she met a short time earlier.

They would eventually have two children: Julia Simadore in 1958 and Allen Randolph in 1961.

Patsy recorded six more songs in 1958, but none of them would be the follow up hit to *Walking after Midnight* either. By summer 1959, Patsy was broke financially, and almost spiritually as well. McColl continued to pressure her to record only songs to which he owned the rights. She continued to fulfill her contractual obligations knowing the songs were sub par.

Finally, in 1960, Patsy's contract with McColl expired, and she signed her own deal with Decca. Free of McColl's smothering, and now associated with the top producers and musicians in Nashville, Patsy's fortunes changed. In November 1960, she went back into the studio to record a Hank Cochran/Harlan Howard song, *I Fall to Pieces*.

As Patsy lay in a Nashville hospital bed recovering from her frightful automobile accident, it climbed to No. 1 on the Country music charts and all the way to No. 12 on the Pop charts.

The Queen of Crossover was back.

In late summer 1961, Patsy entered the studio on crutches and spent four days recording *True Love*, *The Wayward Wind* and *San Antonio Rose*. Her producer, the legendary Owen Bradley, persuaded her to record a song written by unknown, aspiring songwriter Hugh Nelson. He would later swap "Hugh" for "Willie."

Patsy's first-take version of *Crazy* became a No. 2 Country hit and a No. 9 Pop hit in 1962. She followed it up with *She's Got You*. It went to No. 1 on the Country charts and stayed there five weeks before rising up the Pop charts to No. 14.

With her career finally burning white-hot, Patsy maintained a torturous performing schedule most of the following year. There were no fancy custom buses. It was sedans crammed with musicians and towing trailers on the long drives between gigs. It was an ordeal, and Patsy grew to hate it, but understood it was the price of success.

She was rich and she was famous. It was more than what a child from the wrong side of the Winchester tracks could have dreamed, and despite her reputation as "mean as hell and hard to get along with," when the call came to give instead of take, Patsy was ready to give. That call came in March 1963.

On March 2, 1963, Patsy performed at the Boutwell Auditorium in Birmingham, Ala. It was a "Parade of Stars" show that included Charlie Rich, Mel Tillis, Flatt and Scruggs, and Jerry Lee Lewis. For music fans in Birmingham it was, as one local writer described it, "big stuff."

While the concert in Birmingham was all the talk, 750 miles away in Kansas City, Kans., interest in an upcoming benefit show for the widow of popular KCMK radio disc jockey "Cactus" Jack

Call, who had been killed in a car accident, was barely being discussed. The producer needed a star to generate excitement and ticket sales. He called Patsy for help.

Adding her to the bill would fill the auditorium. Patsy agreed to be a last minute addition. So did Hawkshaw Hawkins and Cowboy Copas.

THEY CLIMB ABOARD Piper N7000P on Sunday morning March 3, 1963. It's a single-engine Piper Comanche, owned and flown by Patsy's full-time manager and erstwhile guitar player Randy Hughes. It is a miserable flight in miserable weather, and Patsy is miserable with the flu. Finally, they land at Fairfax Airport at 2 p.m. central time and drive through the cold rain to Kansas City Memorial Hall.

Patsy is the closing act after performances by Copas, Hawkshaw, George Jones, Billy Walker and Patsy's friend, Dottie West.

She strides on stage in a white chiffon dress and launches into her hits. Congested and tired, she is forced to hold one hand to her ear to hear the high notes while clutching a tissue in her other. After struggling through her routine, she apologizes to the audience and finishes the evening with *Life's Railway to Heaven*.

If it is not her best performance, the audience does not mind. They give her a standing ovation, and sincerely moved by the response, Patsy steps to the microphone and tells them, "I love you all." She returns to her hotel, and spends a sleepless night coughing and nursing her cold.

Too sick to eat, Patsy passes on breakfast March 4 and Dottie insists Patsy rides back to Nashville with her and her husband in their station wagon instead of flying. Patsy agrees, after all she is too sick to fly in the cold airplane plus the weather is too bad to fly and getting worse – much worse. She meets Dottie in the hotel lobby, but just before putting her bags in the station wagon, Patsy reconsiders.

"I'm not gonna ride home in the car," she tells Dottie. "I'll wait for Randy. I think I'll get home quicker."

When Dottie insists it is too dangerous to fly, Patsy cuts her off.

"When it's my time, Hoss, it's my time," she says. "If that little bird goes down, I guess I'll go down with it."

Randy spends the day checking with the weather service hoping for better news each time. He does not get it. The weather worsens and eventually he is compelled to cancel the flight and try again tomorrow.

Around noon March 5, Randy calls for the "VFR Flight Weather" to Nashville. A flight conducted under Visual Flight Rules requires weather clear enough to fly the airplane simply by looking out the window.

Isaiah Zamarripa, the briefer on duty, explains to Randy that VFR conditions could be maintained through Missouri, but closer to the front, located near Paducah, Ky., and extending north and south, flight conditions would remain well below safe minimums.

Visibilities are of particular concern for Randy. If fog, rain, clouds, or haze obscures his view out the window, the only way he would know whether his airplane is banking, climbing, or descending would be by carefully reading his instruments – and he's never been trained to use those instruments.

Randy is flying under Visual Flight Rules. VFR allows a pilot who is not trained to fly by reading his instruments to fly simply by looking out the window. It is how the earliest aviators piloted. If a pilot can see the ground, he can tell which way is down and which way is up, and he can tell whether the airplane's wings are level by comparing them to the horizon.

A flight conducted under VFR is not especially problematic as long as the weather allows a good look out the window. But if a VFR pilot can't see the ground or horizon – by flying into a cloud, for example– he likely will become spatially disoriented – a trick played on the brain by the effects of motion on the inner ear when there are no visual clues to help out. In a matter of seconds, he could lose control of his airplane.

VFR pilots flying into weather that obscures their view is one of the leading causes of small airplane crashes. For that reason, the FAA prohibits VFR pilots from flying in weather that will obscure their view.

Despite the dire forecast, Randy decides to make the trip.

At the Fairfax Airport, Randy calls for yet another weather briefing at 1:22 p.m. and Zamarripa provides essentially the same forecast as before. Undeterred, Randy loads his passengers – Copas, Hawkshaw and Patsy – and their bags into the airplane. They depart at 2 p.m. central time without filing a flight plan.

Randy lands his single engine airplane at 3:15 p.m. in Rogers, Ark., 198 statute miles south of Fairfax Airport. It is a short stop, just long enough to fill the tanks with 19.6 gallons of fuel and a quart of oil. Fifteen minutes later, they are back in the air.

Nothing is heard from the airplane for the next hour and 30 minutes. Presumably, Randy is busy with the harrowing demands of flying the plane in turbulent air, low visibilities and occasional rain.

Randy keys his microphone at 4:58 p.m. and radios a call to the Tennessee Flight Service Station in Dyersburg, Tenn. He tells Flight Service Specialist, Leroy Neal, that he is five miles southwest of Dyersburg en route from Kansas City to Nashville. When Neal radios back the current weather conditions and the dreadful forecast for Nashville, Randy decides to land at Dyersburg instead of continuing the trip.

William E. Braese, manager and operator of the Dyersburg Airport, greets the airplane in front of the terminal at a little after 5 p.m. He points the passengers toward the restaurant and Randy toward the Flight Service Station. Randy hopes to get better news while the others get a good meal.

Patsy, dressed in a red pantsuit, shares a table with Copas and Hawkshaw and dines on shrimp and ice tea. Of the three, her star is the most recent to rise into the entertainment firmament, but Copas and Hawkshaw are enjoying sudden resurgences in their already distinguished careers.

Hawkshaw Hawkins

WITH HIS SMOOTH, RICH VOICE, beaded country/western outfits, and the bullwhip he carried as part of his act, Harold Franklin "Hawkshaw" Hawkins had established himself as the epitome of a Country Western Honky Tonk singer. He and his wife, Country music star Jean Shepard, lived the country-gentry life raising Tennessee Walking Horses on their ranch outside of Nashville. It had been a long road to get there.

Born and raised in the mountains of Huntington, W.Va., Hawkshaw claimed he raised money to buy his first guitar by selling rabbits. His got his first break when he won a talent show on his hometown radio station. They offered him a job even though he was only 15. Later, he moved to Charleston, W.Va., and worked at radio station WCHS.

By the time he was 20, Hawkshaw was working regularly as an entertainer in a traveling show, but when World War II started, he shipped out to the Pacific. Even during the war, Hawkshaw continued to perform, occasionally making appearances on radio stations in Manila. Once the war ended, he returned home to West Virginia and settled into a radio job in Wheeling.

He developed his singing cowboy persona and put together an act that included trained horses and rope and whip tricks. Within a couple of years, he signed with King Records, and in 1948 released *Pan American* and *Doghouse Boogie*. They were both Top 10 hits. During the next three years, Hawkshaw had three more Top 10 hits: I *Love You a Thousand Ways, I'm Waiting Just for You*, and *Slow Poke*, and a Top 15 hit, *I Wasted a Nickel*.

He left King Records in 1953 and signed with RCA, but during the six years with RCA he never had a hit. In 1959, Hawkshaw left RCA and signed with Columbia Records. He had one hit for Columbia, a folk song called *Soldier's Joy*, which made it into the Top 15.

In the fall of 1962, Hawkshaw returned to King Records and rediscovered the magic. Shortly, before the trip from Kansas City with Patsy and Copas, Hawkshaw had gone into the studio to record *Lonesome 7-7203*. As he sips his ice tea in the airport restaurant, it is climbing the charts eventually to become his first No. 1 hit.

AT THE FLIGHT SERVICE STATION, Specialist Leroy Neal explains to Randy how bad the weather will be for the remainder of his flight. A front is moving across Tennessee pushing terrible weather ahead of it. Overcast: 900 feet; Visibility: 5 miles; Light rain and fog; Surface Winds of 20 knots with gusts at 31 knots. To drive home the risk of flying in such weather, Neal reads Randy a special advisory for light aircraft. It points out the possibility of moderate to occasional severe turbulence in the area. Then he emphasizes another problem – visibilities will be diminishing quickly with the onset of darkness in the late afternoon.

Randy calls his wife from a phone in the restaurant and gets the best news of the day – the sun has broken out in Nashville. It looks like the front has passed, so the weather should be improving. He gives the good news to the others.

"If you want to stay, we stay," Patsy says, "and if you want to go, we go."

Perhaps her deference to Randy is a result of their relationship. Many believe it is as personal as professional. Copas' relationship with Randy is also personal. Randy is Copas' son-in-law.

Cowboy Copas

LIKE HAWKSHAW, LLOYD ESTEL "COWBOY" COPAS was enjoying resurgence in his career. He had come to the fore of Country music after World War II with a string of hits. They ran out in the 1950s and his career cooled, but by the early 1960s he had begun making hits once again.

Cope, as his friends called him, was born in 1913 in the hills of Blue Creek, Ohio, a speck halfway between Cincinnati and Charleston, W.Va. He quit school when he was 14, and turned his attention to performing; first with a local string band, the Hen Cacklers, and later with fiddle player Lester Vernon Storer, who adopted the stage name Natchee the Indian.

They gained notoriety from winning a Cincinnati radio station contest and spent the next few years performing in the area.

The country was in a depression and times were hard. Cope supplemented his income during the late 1930s by working at a variety of radio stations in the Charleston/Huntington/Cincinnati area, and he put together his own band, The Gold Star Rangers. They made regular appearances at radio stations in Charleston, W.Va. and Knoxville, Tenn. However, Cope's big break came in 1943 when he took Eddie Arnold's place as singer for Pee Wee King's Golden West Cowboys at WSM radio and the Grand Ole Opry.

At the age of 30, Cope had made it to the top of the Country music industry and he intended to stay there. In 1946, he signed a deal to record as a solo artist for King Records. His first song, *Filipino Baby*, was a hit – the label's first on the Country charts. It marked the beginning of period in which Cope put huge hits on the charts with metronomic regularity.

Next came *Signed, Sealed and Delivered* which went to No. 3; followed by *Tennessee Waltz*, also a No. 3 hit; then *Tennessee Moon*, which climbed into the Top 10; and *Breezing*, a Top 15 hit – and those were just for 1948. The next year the hits continued: *I'm Walking with Tears in My Eyes* – Top 15; *Candy Kisses* – Top 5; *Hangman's Boogie* – top 15. Cope hit the charts again in 1951 with the Top 5 single, *The Strange Little Girl*, and again in 1952 with the Top 10 hit, *Tis Sweet to be Remembered*.

Ironically, that is when the fans began to forget Cope.

He stayed with King Records for three more years, but the hits had stopped. He switched to Dot Records, but that did not help. Finally in 1960, he signed with Starday, and after eight years of watching the hit parade pass him by, he was suddenly leading it once again. *Alabam* hit No. 1 and stayed there for 12 weeks. In all it spent eight months on the Country charts and crossed over to No. 70 on the Pop charts.

He continued releasing songs for Starday and charted three more times: *Flat Top*, a Top 10 hit; *Sunny Tennessee*, a Top 15 hit; and, finally, a remake of his early hit, *Signed, Sealed and Delivered*, went back again into the Top 10.

As he walks with the others back to the airplane, his most

recent release is on the verge of climbing the charts to No. 15. Its title is *Goodbye Kisses.*

RANDY RETURNS TO THE FLIGHT SERVICE STATION and explains to Neal that since the sun is shining in Nashville, he intends to continue the trip. Neal reminds him Dyersburg has also experienced brief breaking of low clouds during the afternoon. The sunshine in Nashville would most likely be brief.

In fact, the storms have not passed Nashville. The sunshine Randy's wife saw is meteorological fool's gold – a break in the clouds through which the sun is temporarily shining, a weather event seasoned pilots call a "sucker hole." But the allure of the mirage is irresistible.

Braese fuels the airplane with 27 gallons, cleans the ashtrays, checks the oil and returns to the office just in time to hear Randy tell the bookkeeper, "just talked to my wife and she said the sun just broke out in Nashville, so we're going on."

Braese also tries to persuade Randy to stay over until the weather passes. He points out a line of storms to the east, terrible weather in which to fly under any circumstances, but especially difficult with night falling. For emphasis, he reminds Randy of, "the sparsely settled area where no lights would be visible."

Finally, Braese urges, "Why don't you stay the night?"

"I've already come this far," Randy tells him. "We'll be there before you know it!"

And if the weather gets too rough, he says, he will simply turn the plane around and come back to Dyersburg. The airport does have lights on the runway for landing at night, doesn't it? Brease assures him it does.

Years later Patsy's husband, Charlie Dick, revealed the source of Randy's hubris to *Midwest Today:* "He was so proud of that little plane … he told me a story about a guy that had a plane exactly like that, and was an inexperienced pilot, and got into a storm and decided he would climb over it. Well he went up so high and he seen he wasn't gonna get over it, so decided he would go down and – being inexperienced – he didn't pull the throttle back. Well, the first thing he knows he's going a whole lot faster than that plane is supposed to be capable of withstanding. Of course, he realized it and pulled it back and pulled it out of the dive and saved it, and when he landed, there were just a few wrinkles on the wing. So, Randy thought that plane could do anything."

THAT PLANE WAS Piper N7000P, a single-engine Piper Comanche that Randy bragged had been owned "by Mr. Piper himself." Piper built five different versions of the single engine model between 1958 and 1972. N7000P was built at Piper's Lock Haven, Pa., plant in January 1961, serial number 24-2144.

It is a 250-horsepower, retractable gear airplane capable of climbing at over 1,300 feet per minute and carrying four people at cruising speeds of about 150 knots. Especially attractive to pilots is the Comanche's unbeatable range. Topping off the 86 gallon fuel tanks will give the plane seven to nine hours of flight time.

However, a pilot's skills must match the demands of such a complex, high performance airplane. The Air Safety Foundation studied years of data and concluded:

"Pilot background and experience is always a question … Sixty four percent of serious accidents occur to single engine Comanche aviators new to the breed … If a pilot survives the first 100 to 200 hours in type, the chances of an accident go down dramatically."

The Air Safety Foundation's report took particular note of Comanche crashes associated with bad weather, Instrument

Meteorological Conditions or IMC. The report noted Comanche single-engine airplanes had *twice* the crash rate in bad weather as other similar planes.

"*ASF can discern no mechanical or aerodynamic reason why the Comanche should fare so poorly. The judgment – and, in some cases, the skill – of the pilots involved suggests that it is hard to be humble when you own a Comanche. In a capable cross–country airplane, a touch more humility frequently equates to survival.*"

The ASF study pointed out one last issue, flying the plane at night yields "*similarly poor comparisons.*"

The inescapable conclusion is a formula for grief – a low-time pilot times bad weather times night equals a multiplicity of risks, each compounding the next.

RANDY HELPS PATSY climb into the left rear seat of the airplane at 6:07 p.m. Cope tucks into the seat next to her. Randy climbs across the co-pilot seat and buckles in while Hawkshaw takes the right front seat. Randy cranks the engine. As he taxis to the runway, he calls the Dyersburg Flight Service Station one last time. Again, he is given the dicey forecast.

At the end of the runway, Randy throttles up the Comanche's 250-horsepower Lycoming engine to full power. He will need all of it. Having loaded four souls, their bags and fuel on board, the airplane is more than 40 pounds heavier than its allowable certified gross weight. He releases the brakes and the plane slowly picks up speed down the runway. He pulls back on the yoke and lifts the nose.

As the heavy plane strains into the unstable air of early evening, Randy points it toward a dark line of clouds. He is heading into a witch's brew of bad weather – fog, rain, low clouds and gusty winds mixed in a caldron of darkness. It is a combination that would challenge the most experienced of aviators. His logbook, tucked away inside the doomed airplane, lists his total flying experience: a measly 160 hours.

At 6:30 p.m., Sam C. Ward is working late in the office at his mining company four miles west of Camden, Tenn., when he hears a faint noise above the blowing storm. Is it an airplane? Surely no one is flying in this weather.

Ward's concern is rooted in years of experience in the cockpit. He has been flying since 1940; served as an instructor for the U.S. Air Corps during World War II; and has owned both a crop dusting service and a flight school. A certified commercial pilot, his logbook lists more than 10,000 hours of flight time.

Ward hurries out into the gusty night and hears, somewhere hidden in the low hanging clouds, "a light aircraft go over the building, and from the sound of the engine, it was just above the tree top or not more than 300 feet above the ground. I thought that plane must be lost and trying to orientate by the lights of Camden ... I did not see the plane but could hear the engine which sounded as if it was running perfectly... I heard the engine rev up and saw a white light going toward the ground at approximately a 45 degree angle."

In the cockpit, Randy sees only a vague glow out the windshield as the airplane's landing light illuminates the surrounding clouds into which he has flown. He and the others feel a vague dizziness. In the clouds and darkness Randy can see no horizon and, not trained to use his instruments, he has no way to know he has let one wing drop slightly and the airplane has begun a descending turn – a dead man's spiral.

The rush of air around the plane grows louder as its speed increases, and Randy pulls back the yoke to make the plane climb and slow. Instead, he unwittingly tightens the spiral and forces the plane to descend more steeply. He pulls back harder and the stomach churning grows stronger.

Suddenly, the plane punches out the bottom of the cloud in a steep, full-power dive. As the blindfold of clouds is yanked away, Randy sees the windshield filled with trees. He cuts the engine power to slow the descent just as the propeller strikes an oak. The blade rips free of the hub as the right wing slams into another tree, tearing it from the plane and slinging the world into a vertiginous spin. The plane flips inverted, slams into the ground and disintegrates.

Ward hears a "dull crash, and thereafter, complete silence."

Though he has seen only a dash of light and heard a dull crash, Ward has no doubt what has happened.

He hurries to call Camden Police Dispatcher, Jerry Phifer, who in turn contacts Tennessee Highway Patrol Trooper Troy Odle, who relays the information to the county sheriff. The sheriff and trooper spend the next few hours crisscrossing the back roads, but find nothing.

A Civil Defense team, along with members of the Camden Police Department and the Tennessee Highway Patrol, mount a full-scale search of a rugged area known as Sandy Point at 11:30 p.m. But the difficult terrain, stormy weather and darkness combine to slow the rescuers.

The search draws on through the night.

By the next morning a misty fog has settled over the woods, making it even more difficult for William Jeffrey Hollingsworth and his son, Jeners, as they struggle through the undergrowth near Old Stage Road.

Around dawn on March 6 they crest a small hill and begin making their way down the opposite side when they are stopped dead by a foreboding sight – a section of yellow airplane wing hanging in the top of a tree like an apparition of doom. Below is the grisliest of sights: a muddy, six-foot-deep crater followed by a three-hundred-foot swath of mechanical and human debris – the remains of Randy Hughes, Cowboy Copas, Hawkshaw Hawkins, and Patsy Cline — whose remarkable lives ended on a stormy night in the woods of west Tennessee.

THE FOLLOWING FRIDAY was a dark day in Nashville. The funerals for Randy and Cope were held that morning. Hawkshaw's remains were buried a few hours later. That afternoon, tens of thousands gathered for a public prayer service for Patsy, Randy, Hawkshaw and Cope.

Patsy Cline's remains were brought back to her hometown of Winchester, W.Va., where on Sunday, March 10, 1963, they were interred in a simple grave in Shenandoah Memorial Park.

THE CIVIL AVIATION BOARD, a precursor to the NTSB, investigated the accident and placed the blame squarely on Randy for *"initiating flight in the existing conditions."* In short, Randy was an inexperienced pilot who took his plane and passengers on a flight into weather that exceeded his abilities – he should have known better.

HAWKSHAW'S NEWLY RECORDED *Lonesome 7-7203* rose to No. 1 on the charts after his death and stayed there for four weeks.

Patsy's star continued to burn as brightly in death as in life. Among her many posthumous honors, she was inducted into the Country Music Hall of Fame in 1973 – the first woman solo artist to receive the honor. In 1995, she was given a Grammy for Lifetime Achievement. As the inscription on her grave explains, "Death can not kill what never dies."

Oddities and Ironies

WITH THE CRASH that killed Patsy, Loretta Lynn and musician Billy Walker joined Waylon Jennings and Tommy Allsup in the exclusive club of "those who were supposed to be on the plane."

According to Lynn, she had planned to accompany Patsy on the trip to Kansas City, but at the last minute was offered a job performing for more money that same weekend and cancelled her plans to travel with Patsy.

Walker had planned to fly back with Patsy but took an earlier flight and let Hawkshaw have his seat on Patsy's plane.

There is something prescient about the songs: The last song Patsy sang at her final concert was, *Life's Railway to Heaven*. Her hit record, No. 8 on the charts, at the time of the crash, was, *Leaving on Your Mind*.

Meanwhile, Cope's last hit, which reached No. 15 after the crash, was *Goodbye Kisses*.

Kitty Wells' husband, Johnny Wright, and his singing partner, Jack Anglin, performed as Johnny and Jack. They were one of the Opry's top duos. Jack was killed in a car accident on the way to Patsy's funeral.

Workers sifting through the debris field after the crash discovered Patsy's wristwatch. The hands had stopped at 6:27 p.m.

Cope's daughter, Kathy, suffered perhaps the greatest personal loss in the crash. It killed both her father and husband, pilot Randy.

As Patsy and the others got up to leave the restaurant in Dyersburg, someone dropped a coin in the jukebox and played *Crazy*. It was the last song they heard before boarding the doomed airplane.

Patsy left a will when she died. She had written it in long hand on a Delta Airlines napkin.

Today, Patsy's husband, Charlie, lives in Nashville and is semi-retired. He still works as an independent contractor with a video production company specializing in artist profiles. He is also affiliated with Legacy Inc., which manages Patsy's estate and licenses tribute productions.

Daughter Julie Dick-Fudge also resides in Nashville.

I HAVE NOTHING TO LIVE FOR...

Otis Redding

Died: Dec. 10, 1967, Madison, Wis.

IT MIGHT BE THE COMFORTING DRONE of the motors hanging out there on the wings. The big Pratt & Whitney radial engines will rattle bones standing nearby, but insulated within the cozy passenger cabin at cruise altitude, they are reduced to a muffled roar. It becomes such a natural part of the background that, like the chirping of crickets on a summer night, it goes unnoticed until it stops.

Or perhaps it is the rocking of the turbulence – the hypnotic effect of motion – like bouncing a baby to sleep on your shoulder.

Or maybe he is just worn out from playing his trumpet through three shows the night before.

There is not much chance to rest when you are touring with the hottest R & B band in the world and during the three-hour flight from Cleveland to Madison, Wis., 20-year-old Ben Cauley has been lulled into sleep in the front of the airplane, a nice, deep, peaceful sleep.

Suddenly, he is jolted awake, his body spinning violently. He can barely breathe as the airplane plummets wildly out of control. He reaches for his seatbelt and unbuckles it.

The impact is immediate, deafening and violent.

Then all is quiet and all is dark. As though in limbo, time has stopped. No light. No sound. Only a cold, dark void.

He breaks the surface of the freezing water gasping for air. Grabbing a cushion floating on the surface, he thrashes around. Nearby is the sinking hull of the airplane where, moments earlier, he was warm, safe and asleep.

A lone voice calls through the fog and drizzle. In the distance, his band mate, 19-year-old Ronnie Cauldwell, is struggling to stay afloat. Cauley paddles toward him, but Cauldwell slips below the surface. Farther away, a second voice calls out. It is another band mate, 18-year-old Carl Cunningham. Cauley starts toward him but Cunningham, too, slips beneath the frigid waters.

So, too does the broken airplane and, suddenly, Cauley is alone in the middle of an eerily quiet lake. There are no more voices and there is no airplane. There is only Ben Cauley, blood trickling down his face, treading water in the cold rain and quiet fog.

From the distant shore comes the faint rattling of residents scurrying about the docks, rushing to see what has happened. When they reach him, he will tell them what he alone knows, and still cannot believe – in the frigid water, 45 feet beneath him, the world's greatest Soul singer, Otis Redding, and his band, the Bar-Kays, are dead.

Otis Redding

CHARTERED AIRPLANES, GOLD RECORDS, and million dollar paychecks were a world away from tiny, dirt-poor town of Dawson,

Ga., where Otis Redding was born Sept. 9, 1941.

His impoverished family moved three years later to the Tindall Heights housing project in nearby Macon, Ga., hoping for a better life. His father found work at Warner Robbins Air Force base, and as a Baptist preacher. It was at his father's Vineville Baptist Church that Otis got his first experience singing. He joined the choir and later a gospel quartet. As he entered Ballad Hudson High School, his interest in music grew and he joined the school band as a drummer.

When Otis was in 10th grade, his father became ill and the family's already difficult financial situation grew even worse. Otis quit school to help, taking a succession of menial jobs. He tried his hand as a parking lot attendant and later as a hospital orderly. However, his heart tugged him toward music, and finally, he found a job that would pay him to play. Local radio station WTBB paid Otis $6 an hour to backup gospel groups appearing live every Sunday.

During the week, Otis would sing with local bands wherever he could – parties, clubs and talent shows. After winning one series of talent shows 15 straight times at Macon's Douglas Theatre, Otis was asked to retire from the competitions. His amateur days had flamed out, but his professional career was about to ignite.

Macon guitarist Johnny Jenkins and his young manager, Phil Walden, spotted Otis at the talent show. Jenkins gave Otis jobs as chauffeur and singer. Walden booked Johnny Jenkins and the Pine Toppers, featuring Otis Redding, to play every high school party and fraternity house in the area. Their live performances were immensely popular, but their attempts to produce an equally popular record on the minor Confederate label failed.

Though his record, a Little Richard knock off, *Shout*

Bamalama, was received coolly, Otis's personal life had turned red hot. He had fallen in love with Zelma Atwood and married her in August 1961. They would have three children and adopt a child.

By 1962, the Johnny Jenkins record *Love Twist* had made its way to the offices of Atlantic Records. Atlantic purchased the rights and released it as a single. Even though it was not a hit, it faired well enough to convince Atlantic to send Jenkins and his band to the Stax Record Studios in Memphis, Tenn., for a recording session with the legendary Booker T. and the MG's, the Stax studio band. Otis drove Jenkins to Memphis.

Recording with the top studio band in the world turned out to be an exercise in frustration for Jenkins, but the chance of a lifetime for Otis. Jenkins's session went poorly and ended early. With only a few minutes left on the studio clock, Otis was allowed to take a turn at the microphone. He recorded two songs that day: *Hey Hey Baby*, another Little Richard-style shouting song and a soul ballad he had written a couple of years earlier, *These Arms of Mine*.

Volt Records, a partner of Stax, released the record with *Hey Hey Baby* as the A side and *These Arms of Mine* as the B side. *Hey Hey Baby* sold moderately well around Macon and other southern towns where Otis was known, but after a few months it seemed destined to follow the path to insignificance just like *Shake Bamalama*. Then something unusual happened.

Disc jockeys flipped the record over and discovered *These Arms of Mine*. They liked it better than *Hey Hey Baby* and so did their listeners. Record sales picked up, not just around Macon but also across the country. By May 1963, *These Arms of Mine* had reached the R & B Top 20. Stax signed Otis to a long-term recording deal and assigned Booker T. and the MG's guitarist, Steve Cropper, to serve as Otis' arranger and producer.

At Stax studios, Otis and Cropper developed a working environment bent on capturing Otis' passion, energy and spontaneity.

Otis told *Rolling Stone Magazine*, "At Stax the rule is: whatever you feel, play it. We cut everything together – horns, rhythm and vocal. We'll do it three or four times, go back and listen to the results and pick the best one. If somebody doesn't like a line in a song, we'll go back and cut the whole song over. Until last year, we didn't even have a four-track recorder. You can't overdub on a one-track machine."

Music from the other Soul factory at the time, Motown Records, was polished, orchestrated and tidy. Music from Stax/Volt was raw and powerful. Stax/Volt had begun writing the dictionary of Southern Soul and Otis was its author.

Otis released his first album, *Pain in My Heart* in 1964. Sales were modest but critics noted Otis' remarkable emotional range – shouting a Rock 'n Roll song like Little Richard one moment, singing a tender ballad like Sam Cooke the next.

Now a full-fledged recording artist, Otis struck out on a relentless schedule of touring, punctuated by recording sessions. In March of 1965, he released his second album, *The Great Otis Redding*, another modest success followed by more touring and more recording.

Then in September of that year, Otis shook the R&B world with the release of the astonishing album, *Otis Blue/Otis Redding Sings Soul*. Recorded in a single 24-hour period, it blessed the world with the Soul gems, *RESPECT*, and *I've Been Loving You Too Long*. Also on the album were several cover songs: Otis's high octane version of the Rolling Stones' *Satisfaction* made Mick and Keith seem downright laconic; his version of The Temptations' *My Girl* became a hit in Europe and with *Wonderful World* and the powerful *A Change Is Gonna*

Come, Otis tipped his hat to one of his mentors, Sam Cooke.

Otis Blue was a watershed release for Otis. While his previous albums had been moderately successful, *Otis Blue* marked the first time he enjoyed truly widespread appreciation across the R & B world.

What Otis still did not enjoy was acceptance outside that world. His hits, including *Mr. Pitiful, I've Been Loving You Too Long, RESPECT, Satisfaction, and My Lover's Prayer,* were scoring big on the R & B charts but struggling to break the Top 20 on the broader Pop charts.

Consequently, the song *RESPECT* held particular significance for Otis. Seemingly about a workingman who only asks for "a little respect when he gets home," it is more a metaphor for Otis' view of his career. In the world of R & B he was finding success – respect – but the much wider world of popular music continued to ignored him. It was that broader success, in the largely, young, white, Pop world he longed to achieve.

Still, R & B success was enough to provide Otis and his family a lifestyle far removed from the housing projects of his youth. In 1965, he moved his family to a 300-acre farm in Round Oak, Ga., near Macon. Among the barns and pastures, he built the largest private swimming pool in the state and made plans to build a private runway for his personal airplane. He named the farm, The Big "O" Ranch. However, with his hectic schedule he barely had time to enjoy it.

Between concert appearances and recording sessions, Otis spent much of his time at the offices of his managers, brothers Alan and Phil Walden in the Robert E. Lee building in downtown Macon. The Army had ordered Phil to Germany, so Otis pitched in to help Alan with the office duties.

Later, in a biography for the official Otis Redding Web site,

Alan wrote, "Sometimes he would be traveling and I would arrive at 6 a.m. to open the office and I would discover Otis ... already in the office reviewing the receipts and box office funds from the night before. He would travel a couple hundred miles extra just to work in the office before leaving for his next concert."

Adding to his burdens, Otis began his own production company, Jotis, to nurture the careers of aspiring artists, among them Arthur Conley.

Life on the road had become more difficult as well. Guitarist Johnny Jenkins was afraid of flying, but the demands on Otis' time occasionally demanded it. Eventually, Otis split from his long-time band and began traveling to his concerts alone. He hired local musicians, rehearsed with them during the afternoon and performed with them that night.

He did his best to make it work, but was never happy with the arrangement. Then he saw a band in Newport News, Va. that solved his problem. They had a tight horn section and both a male and female singer. Otis hired them and created the *Otis Redding Show and Revue.*

He piled the entire entourage into an indifferent 1949 Flexie bus and hit the road. Now with his own band and bus, Otis took concert bookings across the country. In a savage onslaught of touring, the *Otis Redding Show and Revue* performed seven days a week. After each concert, they would climb back in the Flexie and try to sleep while the bus grumbled down the highway toward the next destination.

In October 1966, Otis released the album, *Dictionary of Soul*, with a song written 33 years earlier by Harry Woods, James Campbell and Reginald Connelly. Otis turned the simple love song, *Try a Little Tenderness,* into the impassioned plea of a tent preacher revved to full frenzy on a hot August night. His heavily improvised version stunned the R & B world and infused the term "Soul music" with profound meaning – the song seemed to spring straight from his soul.

As the year ended, *Try a Little Tenderness* rose to No. 4 on the R & B charts. Nevertheless, like the rest of his songs, it struggled to gain prominence on the Pop charts.

When 1967 started, it appeared to be Otis' biggest year yet. Having conquered the R & B world, Otis determined to find acceptance – respect – among the broader white audience. And there was opportunity in 1967 to do that.

In the spring, he joined a tour of Europe with other Stax Record artists. The Stax/Volt Tour was wildly successful and solidified his position as a bona fide star in Europe. London's *Melody Maker* magazine named him the International Male Vocalist of the Year, knocking off no less a performer than Elvis Presley who had won the award every year for the previous 10 years.

With momentum on his side, Otis returned to the states for what would be his most triumphant performance. He walked on stage at the 1967 Monterey Pop Festival; a black man fashionably dressed in a green silk suit and tie, and looked out upon a sea of young white hippies in tie-dyes, beads and blue jeans. It was the moment of which he had dreamed – the chance to bring his music – Soul music – to a young, white audience.

He was the last performer of the three-day event. Jefferson Airplane had just finished their show and many were already heading for the gates, but when Otis kicked into his turbo-powered show, they returned to their seats.

It was a rare and defining performance. Otis seemed not so much to perform as to proselytize – the Hell fire revivalist in a Holy Ghost frenzy once again. By the end of his show, the "love crowd" was standing and cheering. Otis had not only broken through to the larger audience he had sought for his career, but also shattered an American social barrier.

Otis had delivered Soul to white America ... and they loved it.

After Monterey, he took a couple of months off for throat surgery and rested on a houseboat in Sausalito, Calif., loaned to him by legendary impresario Bill Graham. There, while sitting in the morning sun, an idea for a song came to him. He returned to Memphis and, with Steve Cropper, finished writing the acoustic ballad that would become his signature hit.

Sitting on the Dock of the Bay was pensive and poignant – the longings of a man down on his luck and a long way from home – not a soulful love ballad or a frenzied soul-rocker of which his fans had grown accustomed. Among some in Otis' inner circle, the reaction to *Sitting on the Dock of the Bay* was less than enthusiastic. However, Otis was steadfast. This was the song that would break through the white-dominated Pop charts to bring him, finally, the wider audience and respect for which he had worked so hard.

Otis recorded his vocal part for *Sitting on the Dock of the Bay* on Dec. 7, 1967, at the Stax studios in Memphis but left the studio before the song was finished. As usual, there was a schedule of shows beckoning. Steve Cropper stayed behind to add instrument parts as Otis left for the airport.

OTIS HAD ACQUIRED one of the perquisites of good fortune – his own private airplane, a twin-engine Beech 18H. The Beech 18H is the final variant in Beechcraft's long run of its Beech 18 model. The original Beech 18 first took flight in January 1937. The military adopted it as a light utility aircraft during World War II and gave it the military designation C-45. Beech produced more than 5,000 C-45s for the war effort and many of them returned to civil service at the war's end. Beech quit building the Beech 18 in 1969 after one of the longest production runs of any model in aviation history.

The Beech 18H that Otis acquired was a good choice for a group of touring musicians. The twin Pratt & Whitney "Wasp" radial engines produced 450 horsepower each, enough to lift a couple of tons of musicians and instruments. It would not set any air-speed records, but it could cruise comfortably at nearly 200 miles an hour. Otis' Beech 18H was configured with seats for the pilot and co-pilot in the front with three individual seats and a couch in the rear passenger compartment.

ON DEC. 10, 1967, the couch is occupied by Bar-Kay band members 19-year-old Phelan Jones and 18-year-old Carl Cunningham and Otis' valet, Mathew Kelley. In the three individual seats are band members Ronnie Cauldwell, 19, Jimmie King, 18, and Ben Cauley, 20.

Band members James Alexander and Carl Sims are not on board. They are escorting the group's luggage and musical instruments on a separate commercial flight. Otis has climbed into the cockpit's right seat and 26-year-old pilot Richard Fraser, a former military pilot, is in the left.

Fraser is chief pilot for Otis Redding Enterprises. He is a husband with two young sons. He has good credentials for the job. He holds a commercial pilot's certificate and is instrument rated to fly both single engine and multi-engine airplanes. He has accrued more than 1,200 hours of flight time with 118 hours in the Beech 18H. At the age of 26, he already had spent eight years in the Air Force and had been released only four months earlier.

Though fully certified to fly the airplane, on the flight from Cleveland to Madison, Wis., Fraser has his hands full. The bad weather – drizzle and fog – forces him to fly the airplane solely by reference to the cockpit instruments.

As he approaches Madison's Truax Field, Fraser begins an instrument landing approach – a series of blind turns and descents that should end with the aircraft breaking out of the clouds a few feet above the threshold of the runway.

Three miles from the field, he radios the airport's tower and tells the controller he is at the Outer Marker, the first of three "check points" he must hit along the final approach path to align the airplane with the runway as he descends through the clouds. It is a point in the air several miles from the runway and several hundred feet in the air.

STANDING IN THE FRONT YARD of his house on Lake Monona, near Madison, Wis., 54-year-old Bernard Reese hears something strange overhead in the clouds. Sounds like an airplane, but something is not right.

From the living room of his lake house, Chris Dickert hears it, too, a low-flying plane that just does not sound right. He gets up to go to the window overlooking the lake.

Suddenly there is an explosion "like an auto accident." Both men, Reese from his yard and Dickert from his living room, see a huge splash in the middle of Lake Monona. When the water settles, they are astonished to see the remains of an airplane floating on the surface.

In the tower at Truax Field, the airplane's "blip" on the radar screen disappears without warning. The radar shows the airplane's last position so close to the airport the air traffic controller is convinced the airplane has crashed on the far end of the field and scrambles the rescue trucks to the end of the runway.

Dickert, Reese and other lake residents scramble to their

boats and telephones to call for help and run to the rescue. Agonizing minutes go by until the first of them arrives in the middle of the lake. By then, the bulk of the airplane has sunk. They find nothing but scattered debris and, clinging to a floating seat, nearly frozen in the 34-degree water, Cauley with his news that will stun the world.

Madison deputies rescue Cauley, then immediately recover the bodies of pilot Fraser and 18-year-old Jimmie King. Both are still strapped in their seats.

LEGENDARY SOUL SINGER James Brown got the word that night while resting in the backstage dressing room during the intermission of his concert at the Memorial auditorium in Nashville, Tennessee. For James and his band, the news was devastating.

"It was like a fire had come through there," he remembers. "We were so down, way down."

As the house lights dimmed for the second half of his show, James walked alone to the microphone and told a stunned crowd, "We just lost a good man, a great artist, a good friend, someone you all loved."

FULL-SCALE RECOVERY EFFORTS began at 7 a.m. the next day. On their second descent of the morning, divers discovered Otis' body, still wearing earphones, a few feet from the airplane. Next, they recovered the body of Mathew Kelley from inside the aircraft. Divers continued searching until dark, but failed to find anyone else. They marked the crash site with buoys and suspended the operation for the night.

Divers recovered the body of Cunningham at 11:30 the next morning, but found no more bodies and spent the next several days retrieving airplane parts, luggage and musical equipment from the lake bottom. Then, just before noon Dec. 20, they found the body of Cauldwell.

Eventually, all the bodies were recovered and examined by the local coroner. He found for the most part only superficial injuries. Astonishingly, many had survived the crash only to drown in the cold waters of Lake Monona.

THE CIVIL AERONAUTICS BOARD investigated to determine why Otis' plane would spin out of control and plunge into the waters of Lake Monona just three miles short of the runway. They never figured it out. The final report lists the cause of the accident as simply: *Undetermined.*

OTIS' BODY WAS RETURNED to his hometown of Macon, Ga., for a funeral at the Macon City Auditorium. Among the 4,500 mourners was a who's who of Soul, including James Brown, Aretha Franklin, Little Richard, Stevie Wonder and Wilson Picket. Distraught fans lined the motorcade route from the auditorium to the gravesite at Otis's ranch in Round Oak, Ga. Some flung themselves onto the stars' limos as they passed.

A few days later, *Sitting on the Dock of the Bay* entered the charts and shot to No. 1, not just on the R & B charts, but also on Pop charts around the world. It went on to win a Grammy for Best Song of the Year and a Grammy for Best R&B Performance. It sold more than 4 million copies and became Otis' first gold record.

OTIS WAS INDUCTED into the Georgia Music Hall of Fame in 1988, The Rock and Roll Hall of Fame in 1989, The Songwriters Hall of Fame in 1994 and was awarded a Grammy for Lifetime Achievement in 1999.

Contrary to the song's lyrics, at the time of his death, Otis had everything to live for – family, fortune, fame and finally – respect.

Oddities and Ironies

THE MADISON COUNTY CORONER determined that many of those who died in the crash survived the impact, but then drowned. Ben Cauley, the only survivor, was the only non-swimmer on the flight.

Ben went on to play trumpet and arrange music for icons such as Isaac Hayes, the Doobie Brothers and the Rolling Stones. Although he suffered a diabetes-related stroke a few years ago, he continues to be musically active in his church and uses his personal recording studio to help aspiring musicians realize their dreams.

Otis was not sitting "on the dock of the bay" when he wrote the song. He was sitting on a houseboat loaned to him by music promoter Bill Graham. "Sitting on a houseboat of the bay" did not have the same ring to it.

Otis never heard the final version of *Sitting on the Dock of the Bay*. After cutting his vocal track, he left to begin a tour before the instruments were added.

Bar-Kay band members James Alexander and Carl Sims belong to that exclusive club of lucky ones who "weren't on the plane." Otis' Beech 18H was not big enough for the entourage's equipment. It was sent to the next stop via commercial airliner. Alexander and Sims flew on the airliner to escort it.

THERE NEVER SEEMS TO BE ENOUGH TIME...

Jim Croce
Maury Muehleisen

Died: Sept. 20, 1973, Natchitoches, La.

HIDDEN IN THE DARK BENEATH THE AIRPORT'S BEACON, plainclothes officers Ronald Dove and Joseph Brossett wait in their unmarked car. Natchitoches, La. Police Chief Harry T. Hyams, Officer Albert Winbarg and Sheriff Deputy Bob Self have secreted themselves nearby behind the Acme Cement Company on Rapides Avenue. It is a drug stakeout and they are wide-eyed for anything suspicious. It does not take long.

Hyams spots him first, a slight grey-haired man in dark trousers and light shirt running south on Rapides Avenue. Why would anyone be running around these parts in the dark of night unless they are up to no good? Then Winbarg notices something particularly strange – he recognizes the running man. Just minutes earlier, as he was leaving the police station for the stakeout, a man acting "nervous" and asking directions to the airport had approached Winbarg. He is sure the man running down Rapides is the same man.

Hyams radios Dove and Brossett. They are watching him too,

running furtively around the rear of the National Guard Armory "like he was looking for something." Dove yells at the suspicious character and orders him over to the car.

The running man approaches, sweating and nervous, and tells the officers he is looking for the airport. He pulls out a handkerchief, wipes his face, and, breathing heavily, explains that he is a pilot, a commercial pilot in fact, and that he has passengers waiting at the airport. He couldn't get a cab from the Revere Inn Motel and his passengers have been waiting since 10:30 p.m., so he decided to walk, or run rather, and now he's lost, and he can't seem to find the airport, and he's late, and he's supposed to fly his passengers to Dallas.

A pilot running around looking for the airport after 10 o'clock at night? Wait until the chief gets a load of this, Dove thinks.

Dove and Brossett drive the running man to the chief's stake-out position and explain how strangely he is acting. They put him in the back seat of the chief's car. The chief has a few questions he would like answered: A pilot, eh? With passengers waiting at the airport? Well, where is your pilot's license? Oh, in the airplane! Well, now that ought to be simple enough to verify.

Convinced there would be no plane and certainly no waiting passengers, Hyams and Self drive the man to the airport. However, when they arrive, they are surprised to find a twin-engine airplane in front of the main hangar and several men shuffling near it. As the running man approaches, they greet him inquiring about where he has been and why he is so late.

Assured that the running man is on the up-and-up after all, the chief and deputy leave him at the airport with his annoyed passengers and head toward the Towne House Restaurant a mile away, laughing that they wouldn't want the strange little guy piloting any airplane they were on. Hyams radios Dove and

Brossett with the surprising news: the running man checked out.

From beneath the beacon, Dove and Brossett hear the plane engines fire up and listen as it accelerates down the dark runway. Seconds later, the roaring engine stops abruptly. There is a moment of silence, then a thud.

Dove and Brossett see nothing in the darkness. Instead of the deafening roar of the twin radial engines, there is now an eerie silence. After a moment Brossett keys the mic on his police radio and calls Chief Hyams, "I don't think they made it. I think they crashed."

Jim Croce

JAMES JOSEPH CROCE WAS BORN JAN. 10, 1943, in South Philadelphia's working class, Italian-American neighborhood. In his early years, the home of James Albert and Flora Croce was filled with music and young Jim soaked it up ... Fats Domino, the Coasters, the Impressions. He later told *Guitar Player Magazine*, "Like all kids in South Philly, I learned to play accordion. By the time I was six, I was shaking the bellows to Lady of Spain just like everyone else."

By his mid-teens, Jim graduated from accordion to guitar. He was inspired by listening to two fellow employees playing the blues in the stock room at the toy store where he worked, so he took his brother Rich's clarinet to a pawnshop and traded it for a Harmony F-slot guitar.

He took it with him when he went to college.

Jim arrived at Villanova at the very moment the Folk music explosion of the 1960s arrived on college campuses and in coffeehouses across the country. When he was 18, he became serious about music, later confessing, "I was a late bloomer."

When he was not working his gig as a Folk and Blues disc jockey at the college radio station, Jim was playing the frat house circuit with a variety of cover bands. His play-what-pleases-them philosophy required him to become proficient across the wide landscape of popular music.

He later told *The Village Voice*, "I'm kinda a musical psychologist or a musical bouncer or a live juke box; it depends on the audience. I've got a book at home where I wrote down about 2,500 songs, songs from the '30s, from the First World War, old ragtime tunes, all the way to *Tennessee Waltz* kinda things, it depends on who's in the place. I've always just tried to bounce off what was happening, in any situation, with any audience. I can do a fine version of *Okie From Muskogee*, you know, I've needed it in some bars I've played."

Some of those songs he learned from his friends and fellow Villanova classmates, among them Tim Hauser, who would later found The Manhattan Transfer, future record producer Tom Picardo, and aspiring folksinger Don McLean.

Mclean later explained in an interview with the BBC, "He heard me play and sing and he wanted to be friends with me. So, he and I got to be friends and he got me a job in the school radio station and I used to have a little radio show where I would play folk records that I liked. We stayed friends for a long time. He wanted to become a child psychologist. Most people don't know that he was very well educated ... I quit school the following year (to become a musician) ... I remember saying good-bye to him and him saying, 'Oh that's too risky for me. I want to go on with my teaching career and so on and so forth.' And I think the fact that he saw me do that kinda made him yearn to break out and become more what he had inside himself ..."

Though reluctant to commit fully to a career in music, Jim

became very interested in committing to Ingrid Jacobson. They met on the snowy night of Dec. 23, 1963. Jim was judging an audition for an upcoming Folk music show. Ingrid was auditioning as part of a show-tune singing group called "The Rumrunners." Jim, 20, was impressed with 16-year-old Ingrid.

She told the *Philadelphia Inquirer*, "I was sitting there in a borrowed white dress with black stripes, black boots, and long black hair, trying to look like an established folk singer. He came up to me and said, 'You look just like a little skunk.' He didn't mean it in a mean way, and he was so upset and embarrassed." Moreover, he was smitten.

The Rumrunners passed the audition, and when Jim and Ingrid met again at the concert a month later, they could not ignore the mutual attraction and began a full-blown relationship.

The following summer Jim won a National Student Association "Embassy Tour" of the Middle East and Africa. Performing before non-English speaking audiences was a defining experience which led him to the realization that "if you mean what you're singing, people will understand."

Jim returned home to finish his degree in psychology and pursue his passion for music. Unfortunately, his passion did not translate into gainful employment and a lean succession of gigs hyphenated a rich succession of jobs. Though well-educated, he worked as a laborer and truck driver, frustrating experiences found to be "steadily depressing, low down, mind messing."

Finally, in an effort to find employment even remotely tied to music, Jim took a job selling ads for a Soul radio station in Philadelphia. He became a one-man ad agency. He would call on the businesses, sell the ad concept, write the copy then produce and record the spot himself. However, he quickly grew weary of producing "jive jingles" and abandoned that job, too.

Then he tried teaching guitar.

Then he tried teaching emotionally disturbed children.

And he continued to try to find some way into the music business. It seemed nothing was working, except his relationship with Ingrid and that had a problem, too.

Ingrid was Jewish. Jim was Italian-Catholic. It was a problem for both families. Eventually, Jim converted and on Aug. 28, 1966, married Ingrid in a traditional Jewish ceremony. Jim invited neither family nor friends, aside from his brother, Rich. His parents boycotted the wedding.

Jim and Ingrid moved to Mexico where she had a grant to study pottery, but did not stay long. Jim's old friend from Villanova, Tom Picardo, had changed his name to Tommy West and started "Cashman, Pistilli and West," a new production company in New York City. Jim and Ingrid were the first act he signed.

In the fall of 1968, Jim and Ingrid moved to New York and by 1969, West had secured their first recording deal with Capitol Records. Finally, success was on the musical horizon. The eponymous *Jim and Ingrid Croce* was released with high hopes. Jim and Ingrid spent the next year relentlessly working the Bleeker Street coffeehouse circuit of Greenwich Village. Despite their efforts, the album generated little interest. A lot of hard work, another dead end.

Frustrated with his career and aggravated by life in the city, a place he "never once felt at home," Jim and Ingrid abandoned both and moved to a farm near Lyndell, Pennsylvania.

Their 18th century farm provided a bucolic retreat. Ingrid baked and canned while Jim did manual labor around the farm and picked up work as a truck driver and construction worker. Musically, he was reduced to occasional work as a session singer on commercials – "mostly ohhs and ahhs" he would later laugh.

Then in September 1971, Ingrid gave birth to their son, Adrian James. The following winter the financial pressures deepened with the snow. So, like a farmer selling his seed corn, Jim sold his guitars, one-by-one to pay the bills. With a wife, son and mounting debt, his music career now was little more than a fading dream and Jim wondered, "What in this world's a poor dreamer to do?"

Maury Muehleisen

IN THE EARLY MORNING hours of Jan. 14, 1949, the doctors came to Margaret Muehleisen with surprisingly good news: her newborn son had arrived with a "caul" – a bit of membrane that normally covers the fetus – on his head. It portends a gifted life. After bringing little Maury back home to the family's row house on South Hermitage Avenue in Trenton, N.J., Margaret and Maurice began to wonder what that gift would be.

Maury did not seem "different." In fact, the only thing that seemed unusual about him the first couple of years was how much he cried. Music seemed to be the only thing that soothed him and Margaret spent endless hours rocking and singing to him. When she put him down to do housework, she was careful to place his playpen by the radio.

As he grew into his second year, Maury's parents became increasingly concerned that his speaking skills were not developing. They read to him regularly and coaxed him to talk, but he had no words – not even baby talk. Aside from "humming" himself to sleep, he was a silent child.

When he was 3, an amazing thing happened – Maury began

talking. Not gibberish or baby talk, but fully developed conversational speaking. It was as though he had known how to talk all along and had simply waited for the right moment. Even more surprising, Maury could recite, verbatim, the nursery rhyme books his parents had been reading to him. Perhaps the doctors were right; Maury was going to be a gifted child after all.

Elvis-mania was in full swing at the Muehleisen house in 1955 and, like so many other young boys, Maury wanted a guitar of his own. However, the Muehleisen family was a "piano" family. Maurice, Margaret and all eight children frequently crowded around the old upright piano in the living room for family "songfests."

A guitar? Who could afford a guitar, especially with a perfectly good piano in the living room? If Maury wanted to learn to play music, his father explained, he would have to learn the piano. But as far as Maury was concerned, Elvis didn't play piano so why should he?

Eventually, Maurice took his own counsel. No sense letting a piano go to waste. Since the family's budget had no room for lessons, he purchased a "teach yourself" instruction book and got busy. One day, as Maurice labored through the pages, Maury came in from playing, stopped by the piano and listened. When Maurice explained that he had learned to play by reading a book, Maury asked if he could, too. Maurice gave him the book with the single admonition to learn each page perfectly before moving to the next.

Maury breezed through the first half of the book then asked his astonished parents for lessons so he could learn the real way to play piano. By the time he was 9, he was ready to master the classics – and reveal his true gift.

In most ways, Maury's teens were not unlike many others. He

attended classes at Cathedral High School, ran his afternoon paper route, and spent endless hours in his upstairs bedroom with his latest 45s and albums.

Though he excelled on piano, it did not lend itself to the Folk songs in which he had developed an interest. So, at the age of 17, he bought a Harmony classical guitar and began to seriously study the songs on his 45s. He would write down the lyrics then bound downstairs to work out melodies and chords on the piano before bounding back upstairs to listen and strum some more.

Suddenly, the Folk songs sounded right. They sounded so right, in fact, he was inspired to begin writing his own - another gift.

As he entered nearby Glassboro State College, Maury switched to a Yamaha steel string guitar and became a "professional" musician, playing in the coffeehouses around Trenton for $25 a night. By the time he was 18, he was an accomplished guitarist, singer and songwriter earning a living, albeit a meager one, doing what he loved. All he needed now was a little bit of luck.

On Feb. 20, 1969, Maury was participating in a college Folk music concert at Glassboro State's auditorium. Maury's friend, Joe Salviulo, an assistant professor of Communications, was impressed with Maury's performance and mentioned that he had a friend in the record business, an old college pal from Villanova named Tommy West. Salviulo explained to Maury that West and his partner Terry Cashman were looking for talent for their new record company.

Quickly, Maury recorded a demo tape of songs and Joe, acting as his manager, took it to Cashman and West. In early September 1969, Maury signed both a songwriting contract and a recording contract with Cashman and West's publishing and recording companies.

Maury immersed himself in the music business that winter,

recording in the studio in New York and traveling down to south Jersey to play gigs closer to home. By summer 1970, Maury's album *Gingerbreadd* – 11 original songs produced by Cashman and West – was ready for release. Now he needed a band to take on the road to promote it.

Salviulo and West remembered another old college pal from Villanova who would be a perfect fit to back up Maury – a guy whose music career, despite his immense talent, had never gained traction. In fact, he had practically given up and was now living on a farm in rural Pennsylvania.

Maury and his new backup guitarist/singer Jim Croce rehearsed their act and hit the road in the fall of 1970. When they were not playing clubs around Philadelphia, they were frequently at Jim and Ingrid's farm singing, playing guitars, writing songs and hanging out. Quickly, they had become more than fellow musicians, they had become friends, eagerly anticipating the bountiful life that awaited them upon *Gingerbreadd's* release.

It finally happened in November 1970. After months of anxious anticipation, Capitol Records released *Gingerbreadd* – and except for their families and a few friends, no one seemed to care. The company pressed only 11,000 copies and sold even fewer. It was a bitter disappointment for Maury. For Jim, well, he found himself "right back where I started, again."

Though *Gingerbreadd* was an unqualified commercial disappointment, it had brought Jim together with his musical soul mate, Maury. The promise of the sound they developed while sitting around the farmhouse's kitchen table – Jim playing rhythm chords with Maury filling the gaps with his uniquely tasteful lead guitar licks – convinced Jim to pick himself up, dust himself off and run head-long toward the music business brick wall he had hit so many times before. And even if it got him nowhere, at least he'd "go there proud."

In the dead of winter 1971, Jim called his old friend Tommy West one more time. He had a new sound. One created by he and Maury during all those late nights around the farmhouse's kitchen table. And he had a new a tape of songs – not *Jim and Ingrid* songs, but *Jim Croce* songs – a solo effort. Among the songs on the tape: *Operator (That's Not the Way It Feels)*, a poignant tale of love lost; *Walking Back to Georgia*, a hopeful going-back-to-the-one-I-lost journey; *Time in a Bottle*, a promise to a love regained.

Two weeks after the birth of his son, Adrian, Jim left the farm and joined Maury and Tommy at the Hit Factory in New York City to begin recording the new album. During the next few months, it developed into a 12-song collection of: Hard luck stories: *New York's Not My Home; Hard Time Losing Man; Box #10;* Love songs: *Operator (That's Not the Way It Feels); Walkin' Back to Georgia; A Long Time Ago; Photographs and Memories; Time in a Bottle;* Songs of hope: *Hey Tomorrow; Tomorrow's Gonna Be Brighter Day;* and two songs that were portraits of Runyon-esque characters and would become a hallmark of Jim's songwriting: *You Don't Mess Around with Jim* and *Rapid Roy (That Stock Car Boy.)*

While Jim, Maury and Tommy were in the studio, Jim's friend from Villanova, Don McLean shot lightning through the music world with the release of his album and hit song *American Pie*. Released in November 1971, his allegorical view of the crash of Buddy Holly, Ritchie Valens and the Big Bopper, reached No.1 in January 1972, and stayed on the charts for nearly four months. It sold more than 3 million copies as a single and 5 million copies as an album.

McLean's more than eight-minute song with its enigmatic

lyrics, reminded the world, and more importantly radio programmers and record executives, popular songs need not be about losing and gaining love, nor two and a half minutes in length.

With the strains of "Bye bye Miss American Pie" still echoing in the national conscious, ABC Records released Jim's album of two and a half minute songs, *You Don't Mess Around with Jim*. *American Pie* notwithstanding, *You Don't Mess Around with Jim* with its tight melodies, interesting stories, and curious characters was an immediate hit. Its infectious title track roared up the charts and had teenagers across America turning up their 8-tracks to sing along with Jim's list of bad ideas involving superman's cape, spitting into the wind and the Lone Ranger's mask.

The second single, Jim's ode to lost love, *Operator (That's Not the Way It Feels)*, quickly climbed the charts, too.

At the age of 30 – ancient by pop music standards – Jim was finally a hit. Ironically, he was more in debt than ever before. The record company had "fronted" him the money to record *You Don't Mess Around with Jim* against future earnings. That meant even though the record was selling millions, Jim's cut was going to pay back the record company.

His only hope for cash was to perform live concerts.

Two hit records made bookings easy. So, in the best tradition of "striking while it's hot," Jim and Maury set out on a marathon concert tour, scheduling more than 300 shows a year.

Don McLean later told the BBC, "He was just getting started (and) the real heat was on and the pressure to be everywhere, everywhere all the time is crazy cause you're establishing yourself and you've got this moment when the spotlight is on you, you've got this moment to be 100 places …"

And one of the places Jim had to be was back in the studio. Between concerts, he recorded his second solo album, *Life and*

Times. ABC released it in January 1973, and it yielded Jim's biggest hit of all. *Bad, Bad Leroy Brown* made it to No. 1 by July 1973 and dominated the charts and airwaves for the remainder of the year. It sold more than 2 million copies and added the phrase "meaner than a junkyard dog" to the popular lexicon.

As *Bad, Bad Leroy Brown* climbed the charts, Jim and Maury continued their relentless touring, crisscrossing the country to play anywhere they could find an audience – large coffeehouses, college campuses, folk festivals. Jim began appearing on television and guest hosted the popular *Midnight Special* concert program. When his song, *Time in a Bottle,* appeared in a television movie, ABC released the poignant love song as a single and it began climbing the charts.

Of course, the record company wanted more songs, so in fall 1973, Jim squeezed into his frenetic schedule more studio time and recorded the album *I Got a Name.* Then, it was back out on the road.

By now though, Jim and Maury could finally see the light at the end of the tunnel. After a grueling 18 months on the road, there was one more tour of concerts to close out the year, and when they finished, Jim and Maury planned a well-deserved vacation. At last, they would have some time to return to their families and enjoy the fortunes for which they had worked so hard.

TO GET TO ALL THOSE PLACES and to get to them fast, Jim chartered an airplane and hired a pilot. The airplane was a twin-engine Beech 18.

The Beech 18 was developed in the mid-1930s. The first one flew in January 1937. As World War II approached, the military pressed many into service as cargo planes and called them the C-45. After the war, Beech continued to develop the airplane and produced a Beech C-18 and D-18. In 1953, Beech introduced the E-18S – the "Super 18." This was the version Jim chartered.

He made an excellent choice. N50JR, as it was registered, easily accommodated the six people (including the pilot) who were traveling on-board. Its two Pratt & Whitney radial engines each produced upwards of 450 horsepower, enough to pull nearly 3,000 pounds of people, luggage and fuel into the air and cruise at about 200 miles an hour.

The pilot was 58-year-old Robert N. Elliot, a veteran pilot with more than 14,000 hours of flight time. He held an Airline Transport certification, the highest level of pilot certification. Roberts Airways, the company from which Jim chartered the plane, had employed Elliot for less than a year. He had been dismissed from his previous job with Rio Airways of Killen, Texas, for poor judgment and pilot technique.

According to a Rio Airways official *"Pilot Elliot on September 1, 1969, while on a scheduled passenger flight, failed to extend the landing gear on a Beech 18 prior to landing. After the propeller blades contacted the runway he applied full power and made a successful go-around. On January 12, 1971, he flew a non-oxygen equipped or pressurized aircraft at 13,000 feet through heavy thunderstorms and icing conditions. Soon after this incident …he was dismissed."*

ELLIOT LANDS THE PLANE at 2:20 p.m. in Natchitoches, La., for a show at Prather Coliseum at Northwestern State University. As the others head to the arena, Elliot has the plane refueled and then goes to the Revere Inn Motel to rest.

About 1,000 students fill the 2,000 seat coliseum, curious to see the craggy face, mustachioed singer they have been hearing so frequently on the radio. Jim begins the show with a couple of light, feel-good tunes: *Rapid Roy (That Stock Car Boy)* and *Workin' at the Car Wash Blues.*

Through the concert he weaves tales of his life – the odd jobs he has had, the strange characters he has met, the dimly-lit bars he has played. He sings his hit *Operator (That's Not the Way It Feels)* for his third number, then more storytelling before *Roller Derby Queen, Lover's Cross, Thursday* and *Speedball Tucker.* Next, he introduces a song he has recently recorded that will be the theme to the new motion picture, *The Last American Hero* and the title of his next album – *I Got a Name.* Another song from *I Got a Name, Top Hat Bar and Grille* is next. Then Jim finishes the show with the clap-and-sing-along *Bad, Bad Leroy Brown.*

The audience is polite and attentive but not Rock 'n Roll hysterical. At the end of *Bad, Bad Leroy Brown* Jim simply says, "See you later" and leaves the stage as the applause dies.

There is no demand for an encore.

It's just another show in a long stretch of shows. But the exhausting run soon will be over. Just a few more stops, then it is home to celebrate Adrian's second birthday. Jim stops briefly to call Ingrid to go over plans for the party then decides to fly to Dallas rather than spend the night in Natchitoches as scheduled.

At the airport Jim, Maury, comedian George Stevens, road manager Dennis Rast and booking agent Kenneth Cortese are shuffling in the dark by the Beech 18, bewildered and concerned. They are ready to leave, but the pilot isn't there. They wait a little longer. Then, headlights appear around the corner and a strange car pulls up with two lawmen and Elliot inside. Elliot, sweaty and nervous, hops out apologizing as the other two identify themselves.

Elliot hurries everyone on board the plane and straps into the cockpit's left seat. Jim climbs into the co-pilot's seat on the right as the other passengers position themselves knee-to-knee in the four facing seats in the rear.

Elliot starts the big radial engines, releases the brakes, and hurries down the taxiway toward Runway 16. Running behind, he has neither filed a flight plane nor acquired a weather briefing. Turning onto the 4,000 feet long runway, Elliot grabs the throttle handles in his right hand and pushes them forward.

The airplane lumbers down the dark runway toward an unpopulated, unlighted area at the far end. Patches of ground fog pass through the landing light as he pulls the plane into the black of night. The air is smooth as the airplane climbs beyond the runway's threshold. Suddenly, the glow of the landing light catches something in the darkness a few feet ahead of the plane.

The passengers are jolted in a deafening collision. Trees rip both wings and engines from the plane, spinning it inverted. It plunges toward the ground, hitting two more trees, demolishing the cockpit and splitting open the cabin. Plowing nose first into an embankment it comes to rest upright at the edge of an unfinished road, crumpled and stripped. Despite a full load of fuel, there is no fire. And there are no sounds – not even the moaning of the dying. They are already dead.

ALERTED BY OFFICERS Brossett and Prudhomme, the police chief assembles the stake out officers at the south end of the airport and initiates a search. Within minutes, they find the crash site along an unopened, newly constructed by-pass. As they approach the wreckage, they discover Elliot's decapitated body on the ground near the cockpit. Shining their lights into the crushed cockpit, they find Jim's body still strapped in the co-pilot's seat, also decapitated. In the passenger cabin, they find the bodies of Dennis Rast, George Stevens and Maury. All died instantly of massive injuries.

The officers begin the routine duties required of their jobs – securing the area, notifying the coroner, and searching the immediate area. It is then they discover in the dark woods nearby the body of Kenneth Cortese, still strapped in his seat. He, too, died instantly of massive injuries.

Ingrid's phone rings at 4:30 a.m. It is her stepmother with the news.

"It's as if I'd known it would happen," she later told Michael Klein of the *Philadelphia Inquirer*. "I know this sounds weird, but given the pace that Jim was living, that was the only way it would stop."

AFTER AN EXTENSIVE INVESTIGATION, The National Transportation Safety Board concluded the obvious: the cause of the crash was *"Pilot in Command – Failed to see and avoid objects or obstructions."*

In short, the plane crashed because it hit trees on take-off. The NTSB draws no further conclusions but does point to some intriguing factors: There was fog and haze at the airport that evening. Could that have hidden the trees from Pilot Elliot's view until it was too late?

Especially interesting is the NTSB view that one factor in the crash was the *"Pilot in Command – Physical Impairment."*

Elliot had severe coronary artery disease. Dr. William J. Reals, Department of Pathology, Memorial Hospital, Wichita, Kansas, examined Elliot's heart and reported *"There is very severe coronary artery disease present ... It is my opinion that the coronary status of this individual was serious and that the possibility of sudden cardiac incapacitation must be considered in evaluating the accident."*

Elliot had run several miles to get to the airport, and when the officers found him he was "acting strangely," "nervous," "sweating," "having trouble speaking" and "puffing" for breath.

Could his behavior have been due to a failing heart that rendered him helpless during take-off? Slumping forward on the control yoke in cardiac arrest would have pushed the nose of the airplane down – into the trees.

There is another possibility to consider. Pilots are typically trained to climb after take-off at either Best Rate of Climb (the speed that will produce the most height in the shortest time using maximum power) or Best Angle of Climb (the speed that will produce the greatest amount of height over the shortest ground distance using maximum thrust available). Whichever the pilot chooses should safely facilitate his egress from the area.

But there is some evidence Pilot Elliot had his own way of departing a runway.

The NTSB reported: *"According to Mr. John W. Shannon, Mangham Airport, Smithfield, Texas, who observed Pilot Elliot depart the airport on numerous occasions, he stated Pilot Elliot would habitually lower the aircraft nose during the initial climb possibly to build up airspeed prior to establishing a climb toward cruise altitude."*

If Elliot lowered the nose to gain airspeed prior to climbing, might he have accidentally kept the airplane too low to clear the approaching trees hidden in the darkness?

Heart attack, poor piloting technique, or low visibilities – regardless of which or what combination was responsible, according to the NTSB, the blame for the crash lay squarely with Elliot. It was his job to see and avoid the trees and he did not.

JIM'S DEATH WAS IMMEDIATELY compared to that of Buddy Holly. It should not have been. Buddy was an established star. Jim's most glorious days were yet to come.

Jim's death led to a birth of discovery. Sales of *You Don't Mess*

Around with Jim soared, reaching No. 1 on *Billboard's* chart five months later. The album he had recorded the week before the crash, *I Got A Name*, was released shortly afterwards and yielded three hits: *I Got A Name, Workin' at the Carwash Blues* and *I'll Have to Say I Love You in a Song.*

He was honored with two Grammy nominations that year. Later, there were greatest hits albums and compilations. All sold well. After driving trucks, working construction, teaching disabled children and selling radio commercials, Jim finally achieved the success of which he had dreamed his entire life.

An ABC/Dunhill promotional statement released shortly before his death announced "Jim Croce proves to be an artist whose capacity for growth seems endless – this is obviously just the beginning – he should be around for a long time to come."

However, Jim seemed to have a different understanding when he wrote what now seems both omen and epitaph, "There never seems to be enough time ..."

Oddities and Ironies

IN EARLY SEPTEMBER 1973, Jim finished recording *I Got A Name*, with its opening line, "Like the pine trees lining the winding road, I gotta name." A week later, he died when his airplane struck trees lining a road. The subsequent publicity made him a household name.

Despite his status as a rising star, Jim died penniless.

Tragedy continued for the Croce family. Wife Ingrid battled 12 years to recover the rights to Jim's royalties. Two years after Jim's death, son Adrian James lost partial eyesight to a neurological disease and Ingrid suffered vocal chord damage during throat surgery.

Today, Adrian is a talented singer, pianist and songwriter in upbeat Jazz. At 50, Ingrid owns two restaurants and three bars in the San Diego area.

Jim was often portrayed in photographs in work shirts, work boots and smoking cigars. The work shirts and boots were legit, but he rarely smoked cigars, except in publicity pictures.

Don McLean encouraged Jim to become a singer/songwriter. In 1972, Don shot to fame with his song *American Pie* about the crash of Holly. A year later, having taken Don's advice, Jim would meet the same fate.

Jim was named to the Songwriters Hall of Fame in 1990. He continues to be snubbed by the Rock and Roll Hall of Fame.

IF I LEAVE HERE TOMORROW...

Ronnie Van Zant
Steve Gaines
Cassie Gaines

Died: Oct. 20, 1977, Gillsburg, Miss.

THEY ARE STANDING IN THE MUCK at the edge of a primordial swamp, drawn from nearby homes by the shaft of light hovering in the distance, beaming down into the thick pines that, along with snakes and alligators, infest these wet lowlands of southern Mississippi.

Squinting into the dusk, they see more lights arrive over the swamp. The sound accompanying those lights – a rumbling "whoomp, whoomp, whoop" – is barely perceptible, but grows louder as they approach, finally becoming a blowing hurricane as the helicopters pass overhead to land in a nearby field.

Other sounds are coming down "Slaughter House Road," the gravel two-lane that leads to the swamp, the distant rumble and wail of vehicles — ambulances, police cars, trooper cars and cars filled with the curious and concerned. Some screech up, others bog down, but eventually, carload-by-carload, they disembark and make their way down to the others standing in the muck, a growing gathering peering at the luminous shaft shining down above the trees.

Those with official responsibilities fling open their trunks and collect their gear. Others, driven by duty, curiosity or larceny, have begun wading through a waist-deep creek into the swamp and toward the light.

Dozens of small groups gather here and there, whispering and pointing. As anxious minutes pass, the gaps between them fill – a steady flow of people, hundreds milling about, gesturing towards the swamp and whispering, "Is it true?"

Rescuers slog through the muddy slush, weaving through the ghostly dancing shadows cast by the brilliant light of the helicopter hovering over the crash site. In the thrashing wind and thunderous roar beneath it, they find a gruesome swath of airplane parts and people — more than two-dozen dead, dying and desperately injured.

They fight their way through the debris and muck to the front of the wreckage, and find the nose cone. Inside, both pilots are dead. Just below the pilot's window is a freshly painted logo that reads, "LYNYRD SKYNYRD."

At the edge of the swamp, car radios blare the bulletin: the hottest touring Rock band in the world, the hard-drinking, hard-living bad boys of Southern Rock, have crashed in a Mississippi swamp. Five people, including founder and front man Ronnie Van Zant, are dead.

Disc jockeys around the world break format to pay tribute. Universally they begin with the mournful guitar of the Southern Rock anthem *Freebird* and Ronnie Van Zant's opening lyric, "If I leave here tomorrow, will you still remember me?"

Lynyrd Skynyrd

IT WAS THE BEST TIME of their professional and personal lives. After years of abusing alcohol, drugs and each other; after years of frenetic touring; after years of both critical success and failure; Lynyrd Skynyrd had reached a peak that surpassed anything that had come before.

Their sixth album, *Street Survivors*, released just three days earlier, had already sold half a million copies and was destined to be their biggest success with fans and critics alike. The world tour they had begun just five days earlier in Statesboro, Ga., was by far their most ambitious and was especially meaningful for Ronnie Van Zant. On this tour, the band was finally going to play Madison Square Garden – Ronnie's lifelong dream. After years of hard work, hard tours, and harder living, triumph – professional and personal – was finally at hand.

It was to be a different kind of tour for Ronnie this time. At the age of 29, the excesses of the road had already weathered him. He had grown weary and unhealthy. With the birth of his daughter a year earlier, his priorities had begun to change. During a break before the tour, he resolved to tone down his legendary over-the-top lifestyle.

This tour there was to be less drinking, few fights, better music, and a slower pace to savor the experience. On this tour the boozing, brawling, raucous band of bad boys would temper their ways and prove that, despite their richly earned reputation as troublemakers, they had made it to the pinnacle of their profession and intended to stay for the long haul. To send the signal, they would call this tour, *The Survivors Tour*.

The Beginning of Lynyrd Skynyrd

THE FOUNDING FATHERS of Lynyrd Skynyrd — Ronnie Vant Zant, Gary Rossington and Bob Burns — met as teenagers at a baseball park in Jacksonville, Fla., in 1964. Ronnie came to the plate and drove a foul ball down the line where Bob and Gary were watching the game. The ball beaned Bob and knocked him out. Fearing perhaps he had killed him, Ronnie ran to his aid. Fortunately, Bob came to and the teens became friends.

It was the first, but certainly not the last time Ronnie would do damage to a friend. Over the years, he inflicted varying degrees of harm upon fellow band members, friends and strangers, including a series of attacks in which he knocked out eight of keyboardist Billy Powell's teeth.

Quickly, the three's common interest in Rock 'n Roll supplanted their interest in sports, and they created the garage band, My Backyard. Over the next few years, the band evolved through various mixes of players and names until, during a local gig in Jacksonville, Ronnie joked with the mostly high school audience that perhaps they should call themselves "Leonard Skinner" as a goof on a high school gym teacher universally despised by the students.

The crowd approved and the name stuck, although it, too, went through various incarnations, before finally becoming, Lynyrd Skynyrd.

As their commitment to Lynyrd Skynyrd jelled, the members moved into a small house, not much more than a shack, near Jacksonville that doubled as their practice space. Because of the cramped quarters, lack of air-conditioning and Florida heat, they dubbed their home/studio "Hell House." Just as the famous "Big Pink" near Woodstock, N.Y. had served as the crucible for blending the talents of Bob Dylan and The Band, the sweltering Hell House incubated the distinctive sound of Lynyrd Skynyrd, and soon, more than just the neighbors would hear it.

By the early 1970s, Lynyrd Skynyrd had become the dominant Rock 'n Roll band in Jacksonville, Fla. After conquering their hometown, it was time to conquer the world. For the die-hard southern boys, the gateway to "The World" was Atlanta.

Atlanta was home to several clubs that fostered the burgeoning Southern Rock scene, much as Greenwich Village clubs had done for the Folk music scene a decade earlier. Music industry executives paid careful attention to bands playing at two Atlanta clubs in particular – Richard's and Funochios. Lynyrd Skynyrd became a regular at both.

In early 1973, producer/musician Al Kooper was looking for talent for his new Sounds of the South record label, so he paid a visit to Funochios. Kooper, a founding member of Blood, Sweat and Tears, enjoyed legendary status inside the music industry for his session work with Jimi Hendrix, the Rolling Stones and Bob Dylan – the distinctive organ intro to Bob Dylan's *Like a Rolling Stone* was played by Kooper.

Listening to Lynyrd Skynyrd at Funochios, Kooper heard what he had been looking for, and missing, in popular music – a raw, rambunctious energy, swagger, and passion.

He signed them to a record deal and took them to Studio One, the recording studio of the Atlanta Rhythm Section in the Atlanta suburb made famous by their song *Doraville*. There, during 1973, Lynyrd Skynyrd recorded their first album, *Lynyrd Skynyrd (pronounced leh-nerd skin-nerd)*. With songs like *Gimme Three Steps*, *Simple Man* and the instant classic *Freebird*, the album affixed Lynyrd Skynyrd in the firmament of Rock 'n Roll stardom. The boys from the ball field had hit a Grand Slam.

To promote the album, Lynyrd Skynyrd climbed into their van and hit the road for a relentless schedule of concerts. *Freebird* stopped the show night after night, even though it had not been released as a single. Radio stations picked it up and when it finally was released in 1974, it rose to No. 19 on *Billboard's* Singles chart. With their songs now being played on the radio, Lynyrd Skynyrd began playing venues considerably bigger than the bars to which they were accustomed. The venues were about to become even bigger – much bigger.

The legendary British Rock band The Who was preparing a world tour to promote their album *Quadrophenia* and needed an opening act. Al Kooper convinced The Who's leader, Pete Townsend, that Lynyrd Skynyrd would be a perfect fit. The traditionally energetic crowds who came to see the incendiary smash-the-amps and kick-over-the-drums show of The Who first would be treated to the kick-ass, three guitar assault of the baddest, up and coming Southern Rock band in the world.

The tour opened at the Cow Palace in San Francisco before 18,000 people, 10 times bigger than any audience they had ever had.

As Ronnie later put it, "We were shittin!" And fighting. When one of The Who's security men tried to eject keyboardist Billy Powell from backstage – he had his "all access" pass in his pocket instead of hanging around his neck – Powell fought back.

Years later, he recounted his version of the event for writer Marley Brant's book, *Freebirds, the Lynyrd Skynyrd Story:* "(Legendary producer) Bill Graham came running down the stage, down this ramp from the stage and punched me in the mouth, I mean with full momentum. Knocked me about 10 feet. He knocked me silly. I was bleeding everywhere, and I was about to pass out. I showed (the pass) to him, and he finally realized that (it was) people playing with Skynyrd he'd just hit. He apologized; I swear to God, 10 times, sent flowers, even after the tour he sent me flowers at home, apologizing. We became real good friends after that, laughed it off and all that."

Powell is surely one of the few people with the distinction of having been popped in the mouth by both one of Rock's great front men – Ronnie – and by Rock's greatest impresario – Bill Graham.

The 12-city tour with The Who proved to Van Zant and company that they could play with the big boys. Just as important, it introduced Lynyrd Skynyrd's raw and raucous live performances to a new audience of converts, all of whom seemed to rush out and buy the band's album.

Al Kooper took the band to the prestigious Record Plant in Los Angeles to record their sophomore effort. It was generally well received even though some critics felt it did not live up to the promise of their first.

What no one could deny, though, was the star power of one particular song on the album. With it's unmistakable guitar introduction and Ronnie's order to the sound engineer in the booth to "turn it up!" (Which Kooper left on the track for verisimilitude and which later became a standard bit of audience participation at live performances). *Sweet Home Alabama*, Ronnie's frontal assault on Neil Young in defense of southern honor, became Lynyrd Skynyrd's first monster hit, eventually rising to No. 8 on *Billboard Magazine's* singles chart. It also galvanized their public image as Southern Rockers.

When *Sweet Home Alabama* was released in summer 1974, the band was already back on the road, and though on the cusp of Rock stardom, they were still traveling show to show like a band of southern rednecks – in vans, at least for part of the tour.

Because it was going so well, additional dates were added in Europe, and for the first time the members of Lynyrd Skynyrd boarded an airplane for a series of wildly successful concerts overseas. They returned in winter 1974 and spent the rest of that year traveling state-to-state, city-to-city and hall-to-hall in a chartered bus. It was a grueling, non-stop tour of the United States, but it paid off professionally.

They had begun as an opening act, but by the end of the tour, they were headliners. Still, the close living conditions, frenetic pace and relentless travel took its toll on two members of the band.

Bob was first to leave.

Artimus Pyle replaced Bob just in time for the band's first Top 10 album, 1975's *Nuthin' Fancy*, with the hit *Saturday Night Special*. The song's anti-handgun message caught some fans by surprise. Who would have thought the hard-drinking, fast-fisted Ronnie would be a gun control advocate?

Kooper added an eerie moog synthesizer effect to conjure a subtle image of death. Ronnie told acquaintances he liked the effect because it sounded like a plane crash.

In typical Skynyrd fashion, rather than take time off to make the album, they simply made what had now become known as the "Torture Tour" even more torturous by recording the album while continuing to tour – 16-hour days, performing, writing, recording and crisscrossing the country in their chartered bus. As Ronnie had lamented, "… big wheels keep on turning."

Dismayed that *Nuthin' Fancy* only gave them one hit single, albeit, a huge one, the band released its fourth album, *Give Me Back My Bullets*, as a deliberate attempt to make an album that would give them more hit songs.

(In *Billboard Magazine*, the music industry magazine that tracks record sales, a song that is rapidly climbing up a chart is noted with an icon called a "bullet.")

By 1975, the cumulative effects of life with Lynyrd Skynyrd had become too much for guitarist Ed King. Toward the end of the tour he was finished with the frantic pace, the spontaneous fights, and of course, the traveling – the relentless, unending, water torture of bus-to-hotel-to-car-to-venue-to-bus-to-hotel-to-car-to-venue ad nauseum – all part and parcel of life with this road warrior band of Southern Rockers. If he never saw another white line disappear beneath the bus, that was OK with him, and in May 1975, after a particularly bad performance at Pittsburgh's Syrian Mosque, King left and never spoke to Ronnie again.

The band continued for nearly a year without him.

Lynyrd Skynyrd built its distinctive sound around the triple guitar assault of "The Guitar Army" – Ed, Allen Collins and Gary. With Ed gone, they were one guitar short, a particularly vexing problem by summer 1976. The band was preparing to record a series of concerts at Atlanta's famed Fox Theatre for a "Live" album. Backup singer Cassie Gaines insisted the band should give her brother, Steve, an audition. He was an accomplished player, she said. Furthermore, he would fit in well with the other members of the band.

Eventually, and mostly to placate Cassie, they agreed to give him a shot, but it was to be an audition like no other.

Steve and Cassie Gaines

BROTHER AND SISTER, STEVE AND CASSIE GAINES grew up in Miami, Okla., stereotypically small town kids, with stereotypically big time dreams. For young Steve, those dreams got even bigger after a trip to Kansas City to see The Beatles. From that moment on, 14-year-old Steve's guitar became an appendage and he made it clear to all that he wanted to be a professional musician. He played with a variety of regional bands and even made a recording at the famed Sun Studios in Memphis. Still, the "big time" eluded him.

However, while Steve was paying his dues in Oklahoma, Cassie's dream came true. When Lynyrd Skynyrd sought to expand their sound by adding a trio of female backup singers, they chose Jo Jo Billingsley, Leslie Hawkins and Cassie Gaines. The "Honkettes" as they were called, quickly became permanent fixtures with the band.

Members of Lynyrd Skynyrd were skeptical about Cassie's claim that her brother could hold his own with Allen and Gary. They were, after all, two of the hottest Rock 'n Roll guitarists on the planet. Still, they reluctantly agreed to give her brother an audition during a concert stop in Kansas City. Not a private audition, but one in front of a coliseum of fans.

On May 11, 1976, Steve Gaines joined Lynyrd Skynyrd on stage for the song *T for Texas*. Earlier, band members had hedged their bets against the possibility Steve was incompetent – they told the sound engineer that as a courtesy to Cassie they were going to let her brother join them on stage, but if he was no good, to turn off his guitar. It was not necessary. Cassie was right and Ronnie offered Steve a permanent job as a member of Lynyrd Skynyrd's Guitar Army.

STEVE'S PRESENCE INFUSED the band with a renewed enthusiasm as they recorded a series of concerts at the Fox Theatre in Atlanta for the live album *One More from the Road*. It was wildly popular, although critics were quick to point out it drew mostly on songs from early in the band's career, not more recent material. Still, suddenly things were going well again and a reinvigorated Lynyrd Skynyrd returned to the studio in April 1977 to record *Street Survivors*. Even before it was released Oct. 17, 1977, it had sold more than 500,000 copies.

Lynyrd Skynyrd was again on top and, for the upcoming tour to support the album, they would travel in appropriate style.

Gone were the days of grueling hours in cramped tour buses. More recently, the band had been traveling in entertainer Jerry Lee Lewis' 1948 Convair 580 Prop Jet, but before the tour began, the deal for that airplane fell though. So at the last minute, the band settled instead on the Convair 580's lesser cousin, a piston engine 1947 Convair 240. To sweeten the deal, the company, which leased the plane to the band, painted the Lynyrd Skynyrd logo on the nose cone.

In addition, there was another change. Lynyrd Skynyrd's regular pilot, Les Long, was not available, so the band interviewed more than 30 pilots and settled on Captain Walter Wiley McCreary, 34, an experienced pilot who had logged more than 6,800 flight hours, 68 of which were in Convair aircraft, and First Officer William J. Gray, Jr., 32, a fully qualified commercial pilot with nearly 2,400 flight hours, of which 38 were in the Convair.

WHEN IT ROLLED OFF THE ASSEMBLY LINE 30 years earlier, the Convair 240 was considered a state-of-the-art aircraft. After World War II, American Airlines wanted a new airplane to replace the venerable DC-3. So, they approached Consolidated-Vultee Aircraft Company with the specs they demanded: a pressurized cabin, 2 engines and 40 passenger seats (thus the 2-40 designation.)

The Convair 240 is an all-metal airplane except for the rudder and trailing edges of the elevator, which are fiberglass. Unlike the DC-3, it has a pressurized cabin (the first for any twin-engine airliner) and tricycle landing gear.

A pair of powerful 18-cylinder Pratt & Whitney engines, producing 2,500 horsepower each, hang on the wings. The engines have enough power to pull the plane up to 20,000 feet and push it through the air at a cruising speed of 280 miles an hour. It was an impressive airplane and American Airlines immediately ordered 100 of them at an initial price of $316,000 each.

The one Lynyrd Skynyrd leased 30 years later was serial number three.

ON OCT. 19, 1977, the loud "bang" scared the bejeezus out of everyone and sent security chief Gene Odum rushing through the cabin to the cockpit. The airplane was barreling down the runway at Lakeland, Fla., with the piston engine on the right wing spewing a 10-foot torch of orange flame. Odum wanted to know whether he and the passengers whose safety was his responsibility – nine members of the band, 13 members of the crew and a TV crewmember who was tagging along – were about to die.

As he recounted years later in his book, *Lynyrd Skynyrd, Remembering the Free Birds of Southern Rock*, he shouted at the pilots, "There's fire shooting out from the right engine. You have to turn around and go back!"

"There's nothing wrong," one of the pilots said.

"I'm telling you there's something wrong. I saw flames coming out of the engine."

"There's nothing wrong. Go back to your seat and stay put 'til we're in the air."

Figuring the pilots must know best – they were after all, pilots

– Odum returned to the cabin and, like everyone else on board, spent the rest of the white-knuckled flight from Lakeland, Fla., to Greenville, S.C., staring out the window at the starboard engine, as it backfired and spit flames out the exhaust.

The flight had unnerved the entire band. Something was obviously wrong, and the 95-city World Tour had only just begun.

The band played their concert at Greenville Memorial Auditorium that night, then retired to the nearby home of drummer Artimus, whose wife served an after-show vegetarian spaghetti dinner. It was a familial gathering and an especially happy one for co-pilot Gray, who that night confided in Artimus, "I have fulfilled my life's dreams. I have driven an 18-wheeler and flown the world's greatest Rock 'n Roll band."

Despite the convivial atmosphere, concern over the airplane and the next day's flight to Baton Rouge dominated the thoughts of the band and crew. Cassie and Allen went so far as to make reservations on a commercial flight, and then changed their minds.

Eerily, back-up singer Jo Jo Billingsley, who was to join the band a few days later, called to warn about a dream she'd had in which the band had crashed in an airplane. Finally, tour manager Ron Eckerman and the band's assistant Dean Kilpatrick promised to extract from the pilots an assurance the plane was safe.

The next day, Kilpatrick and Odum find the pilots checking the airplane. The captain explains there is a small problem with the right engine's magneto – part of the ignition system – but it is nothing to be concerned about and, even if it was a real problem and the engine quit, heck, they would still have the other engine to take them home. But, he reassures them, to be safe, the leasing company will have a mechanic meet them in Baton Rouge to check the plane. The pilots add 400 gallons of fuel to the plane's tanks, board the band and crew, and then file their flight plan, listing among other things: five hours of fuel on board – more than 900 gallons.

Just after four in the afternoon, the Lynyrd Skynyrd band departs Greenville Downtown Airport for the almost three-hour flight to Baton Rouge, La. The take-off seems normal enough, but soon the right engine begins to labor. The pilots switch it from "auto-lean" to "auto-rich" – increasing the fuel flow – and the engine smoothes out. By now, the airplane has so unnerved the band they huddle for an emergency on-board meeting and make a pact – as soon as they land in Baton Rouge they will arrange to purchase a Lear Jet for the band and a new bus for the crew. They seal the deal with a "huddle handshake" like ball players before a game.

Artimus and Allen are enjoying the sunset with the pilots in the cockpit as the plane begins its initial descent toward Baton Rouge. In the darkening cabin, passengers are variously sleeping, chatting quietly or playing cards. All seems well when at 6:39 p.m. the air traffic controller in Houston, who is now handling the flight, clears McCreary to descend from 12,000 feet to 6,000 feet. Twenty-five seconds later, McCleary radios a routine response.

"We're out of one two thousand for six thousand."

Seconds later, without warning, the comforting drone of the radial engines becomes a heart-stopping silence as both engines sputter and quit. Those snoozing jolt awake, the card game stops and the soft chatting ends, sentences unfinished.

Co-pilot Gray turns to Artimus and tells him pointedly, "If you want to live, you'd better get back there and buckle up." McCreary keys the mic.

"We need to get to a (sic) airport, the closest airport you've got, sir."

Suspecting trouble, the air traffic controller asks the crew whether they have an emergency.

"Yes, sir. We're low on fuel and we're just about out of it, we want vectors to McComb (Miss.), poste haste please, sir."

The air traffic controller advises McCreary at 6:42 p.m. to turn the plane to a heading of 025 degrees – north, northeast. McCreary has flown beyond McComb, Miss., the nearest airport, and must turn the airplane around.

Long seconds pass without word from the Convair. Finally, an inexplicable radio call at 6:44 p.m.

"We are not declaring an emergency, but we do need to get close to McComb as straight and good as we can get, sir."

In his book, *Lynyrd Skynyrd, Remembering the Free Birds of Southern Rock*, Odum recounts dropping his cards and running to the cockpit. "What the hell is going on? I asked.

"'We've got fuel problems,' McCreary called out over his shoulder, his confidence obviously shattered. 'We're going to have to make a crash landing. Get back in your seat.'"

McCreary keys the mic again at 6:45 p.m.

"Center, five victor Mike.... we're out of fuel."

"Roger, understand you're out of fuel?"

"I'm sorry; it's just an indication of it."

The crew does not explain what that indication is. Seconds later the air traffic controller requests the Convair's altitude.

"We're at four point five." (4,500 feet)

The controller tries to contact the Convair several more times but gets no response. McCreary and Gray are too busy trying to manhandle an aircraft that has just lost all power.

They also have lost precious altitude turning the plane around and now there is no hope of gliding to the airport at McComb. But in the gloaming, they make out an opening near a swamp and aim for it. They set the plane on a 5-degree glide slope similar to a normal landing, but with both engines silent there is little else normal about this doomed descent.

In the darkness behind the pilots, the passengers prepare for the worse. Seatbelts are buckled except for Ronnie's. He, with the aid of a sedative, is asleep on the floor, oblivious to his impending doom.

Odum remembers grabbing him, throwing him into one of the large, swiveling "captain chairs" with which the passenger compartment has been retrofitted, frantically buckling his seat belt and screaming in the waking rock star's face, "The plane's gonna crash!"

The tops of the pines strike the fuselage with the fury of a million angry baseball bats. The Convair skims the trees for more than 100 yards then slams into the swamp with such force every passenger seat but one breaks from the floor, launching the passengers, tables and chairs toward the front of the plane. As it skids through the swamp, the huge pines rip both wings and a large piece of the tail from the fuselage. The violence cracks the plane in half, opening gapping holes. And as it comes to rest, the rear third of the passenger compartment is broken at a sickening 90 degree angle to the front.

The swamp is silent except for the occasional moan of the living. McCreary and Gray are still strapped in their cockpit seats, decapitated. Behind them, in the front of the cabin, lies a pile of broken people, tables and chairs.

At the bottom are guitarist Steve, his sister, Cassie, Dean and Ronnie. All are dead.

Artimus, the cartilage torn from his ribs, pulls himself from the wreckage and considers the unspeakable horror around him – six friends dead, 20 badly hurt, the airplane destroyed, deep in a snake-infested swamp upon which night is quickly falling. He hobbles from the wreckage and into the swamp. With single-minded determination and barely able to breathe, he wades through the neck-deep black water, stumbles over a wire fence and finally makes his way to a gravel road toward a farmhouse in the distance.

Crew members Marc Frank and Kenneth Peden, Jr., badly injured but ambulatory, have also left the crash and are following behind Artimus, shouting for him to wait up. He is focused on the distant farmhouse and continues, unaware its owner, suspicious of this bloody, muddy, wet stranger stumbling up the road, has him in the crosshairs of a .30 caliber deer rifle.

Artimus, having ignored the warning shot, brushes the astonished farmer aside and without a word walks into the house and directly to the phone. When his wife, Pat, answers he tells her, "We've just crashed. People are dead. You're gonna see it on the news."

Keyboardist Billy, his nose torn almost completely from his face, pulls himself from beneath the debris and struggles through the wreckage toward the remnants of a wing.

Billy pulls himself onto the broken wing and sits quietly bleeding amid the carnage, unable to comprehend the horror visited upon his band, his friends. With the swamp growing dark and too badly hurt to move there is nothing to do but wait.

IN THE DIM RECESSES of the Air Traffic Control Center in Houston, an air traffic controller is staring at an empty radar screen and growing increasingly concerned. The airplane he has been handling is low on fuel and, suddenly, he cannot reach the pilots by radio. As he tries repeatedly to contact them, another pilot flying near the crash radios to say he is picking up a weak signal from an Emergency Locator Transmitter – known as an ELT – a radio that broadcasts an emergency beacon. It can be activated either manually or by impact forces.

The Air Traffic Controller sounds the alarm, and a military operation scrambles into action.

The U.S. Coast Guard Station at New Orleans notifies an airborne HH3F helicopter of the accident at 6:55 p.m. Within 30 minutes, the helicopter arrives in the general area of the swamp, picks up the ELT and locates the wreckage at 7:36 p.m. The helicopter hovers 25 feet above the trees at the crash site and illuminates the area with its powerful spotlight.

A Coast Guard helicopter loaded with medics, communications equipment, and medical supplies lands near the crash. It is joined five minutes later by a second helicopter crammed with rescuers and gear. At 8:10 p.m. a Coast Guard C-131 "Samaritan" arrives and orbits over the crash site assuming on-scene command.

Area emergency services are notified and Pike County Civil Defense, Pike and Amite Counties Sheriff's departments, Mississippi Highway Patrol, and Southwest Mississippi Regional Medical Center jointly implement their disaster plans. At the scene, six medical doctors, and 20 corpsmen and emergency medical technicians treat the survivors.

For the next three and a half hours, they extricate the band and crew from the wreckage; diagnose and stabilize them; then carry them through the swamp to helicopters or ambulances to be transported to any of five hospitals standing by to receive them. Later, the National Transportation Safety Board would say without the exemplary performance of the rescue workers most of those on board would have died that night in the swamp.

As the survivors began their long recoveries, the National

Transportation Safety Board began its investigation into what caused the crash.

The central question was astonishingly simple: Why would an airplane run out of gas? The facts would prove more mysterious than enlightening.

The problem is one of simple math, and the numbers do not add up. In its investigation the NTSB added the receipts for all the fuel stops the airplane made from the beginning of the tour in Addison, Texas, to the last stop in Greenville, S.C., then subtracted the amount of fuel burned in the hours flown and concluded that over an hour's worth of fuel should still have been in the tanks when the engines stopped.

As the NTSB reported, *"Best estimates indicate that 207 gallons of fuel should have been on board at the accident site."*

However, both of the airplanes tanks were empty. The NTSB analyzed three explanations. *"First, there could have been a fuel leak. However, there was no evidence of a fuel leakage, such as stains or loose fuel tank caps or lines, found in the wreckage. Although this possibility cannot be discounted completely, because there is a remote possibility that leakage evidence could have been obliterated at impact, the Safety Board does not believe it to be the most viable explanation.*

"Second, the aircraft may not have been fueled with the amount shown on the fuel slips. The Safety Board considers this explanation relatively remote because the fuel meters on refueling trucks cannot be reset and, if functioning properly, will reflect the total amount of fuel dispensed to a given aircraft.

"Finally, the engines or an engine could have been burning more fuel than specified and more than the flight crew expected to be burned...operating an engine in the auto-rich configuration would increase the fuel consumption by about 25 gallons per hour for that engine, from 183 gallons

per hour to 208 gallons per hour. During the accident flight of 2.8 hours this would have amounted to about 70 gallons."

But even with the right engine in the "auto-rich" configuration, the NTSB calculates the total fuel burn for the final flight would have been only 583 gallons. If the airplane left Greenville, S.C., with more than 900 gallons on board, as the pilots indicated in their flight plan, there should have been 317 gallons on board when the plane crashed. Obviously, there was not and the NTSB was never able to determine why the pilots listed fuel-on-board as 5 hours in their flight plan. The numbers do not add up.

A complete explanation as to why the airplane ran out of gas just minutes short of its destination might lie with information we will never have. During the final flight, the pilots told Artimus, who happens also to be a licensed pilot, they had switched the troublesome right engine from "auto-lean" to "auto-rich" to help it run more smoothly.

As the NTSB noted in its report, in the auto-rich configuration the engine would burn 25 gallons per hour (208 gallons per hour) more than in the auto-lean configuration (183 gallons per hour). But even that would not have burned enough additional fuel on the final flight to run the tanks dry. So, the question becomes: how long had they run that engine on auto-rich? In addition, did they factor the increased fuel burn into their fuel management calculations? The only people who know the answers, McCreary and Gray, died in the swamp.

The NTSB concluded *"It is impossible to determine how long the aircraft was operated in 'auto-rich,' but it was evidently long enough to exhaust the fuel on board the aircraft."*

Then the NTSB blamed the pilots.

"The crew was either negligent or ignorant of the increased fuel consumption because they failed to monitor adequately the engine

instruments for fuel flow and fuel quantity. Had they properly monitored their fuel supply and noted excessive fuel consumption early in the flight, they could have planned an alternate refueling stop rather than attempting to continue flight with minimum fuel. In addition, the Safety Board believes the pilot was not prudent when he continued the flight with a known engine discrepancy and did not have it corrected before he left Greenville."

DEAN WAS LAID TO REST in Arlington, Fla.

Steve and Cassie were memorialized in their hometown of Miami, Okla.

On Oct. 25, 1977, Ronnie was laid to rest in Jacksonville's Memorial Gardens. It was a simple, private service. Merle Haggard's *I Take A Lot of Pride in What I Am* played in the background, and Charlie Daniels sang *Amazing Grace.* Keyboardist Billy, who had lost so many teeth over the years to Ronnie's temper, was the only band member sufficiently recovered to attend.

On the way to the funeral, Daniels wrote a poem. Reciting it became his standard response when asked to comment on the life of his friend Ronnie.

> *A brief candle, both ends burning*
> *An endless mile, a bus wheel turning*
> *A friend to share the lonesome times*
> *A handshake and a sip of wine*
> *So say it loud and let it ring*
> *That we're all part of everything*
> *The present, future and the past*
> *Fly on proud bird, you're free at last.*
> — Charlie Daniels

Oddities and Ironies

UPON HEARING THE WARNING that the airplane he was on was about to crash, drummer Artimus surely felt the hand of destiny on his shoulder. Both his father and father-in-law had died in airplane crashes.

Lynyrd Skynyrd guitarist Ed was not on the final flight. He had dropped out of the band months before and was replaced by Steve. While visiting Steve's grave, Ed was shocked to learn they were born on exactly the same day, month and year.

Neil Young, of whom Ronnie had written scathingly, "Southern Man don't need him around anyhow," learned of Ronnie's death while performing a concert of his own the night of the crash. He stunned the audience with an impromptu rendition of *Sweet Home Alabama.*

Twenty-three years after the crash, the graves of both Ronnie and Steve were vandalized. Their remains have since been moved to unmarked burial sites.

In 1986, guitarist Allen Collins became paralyzed from the chest down following a tragic car accident. He passed away in 1990 from pneumonia brought on by diminished lung capacity due to his paralysis.

Drummer Artimus Pyle lives in Asheville, N.C., and continues to play music throughout the Southeast.

The airplane rescuers used as a command and control center orbiting above the crash site was a C-131 "Samaritan." It is the Coast Guard's version of a Convair 240. The same type of airplane that brought the band to grief also helped save them.

Lynyrd Skynyrd lives on today with original members Gary Rossington (guitar) and Billy Powell (keyboards). Other bandmates include Ean Evans (bass), Rickey Medlocke from Blackfoot (guitar), Hughie Thomasson from The Outlaws (guitar), Johnny Van Zant (vocals), and Michael Cartellone (drums). Dale Krantz Rossington and Carol Chase sing background vocals.

TO SMILE AND DO MY SHOW...

Rick Nelson
and the Stone Canyon Band

Died: Dec. 31, 1985, near Dekalb, Texas

LATE AFTERNOON ON THE LAST DAY OF THE YEAR, schoolteacher Debbie Foster is playing dolls with her two-year-old daughter, Tiffany, in their rural farmhouse. Without warning, Tiffany begins to cry. A low rumble, she says, is hurting her ears. Probably just a big truck coming down the country road, Debbie reassures the child, but the noise grows louder and, suddenly, the entire house shakes from a deep thunder. Foster jumps up and is stunned to see the window filled by the landing gear of a roaring airplane falling from the sky just feet from her roof, billowing smoke and dripping fire.

It clips two poles by the road, hits the ground, and careens toward a pasture of scattering cows. Trees shear the wings down to the engine nacelles and slow the plane's roll until finally it lumbers to a smoking halt. Foster can't believe what she's sees: In the field across the road a large cargo plane sits perfectly upright on its landing gear, stubs for wings, the left prop still spinning, and smoke spewing furiously from the fuselage. It is then she realizes her own yards, front and back, are on fire.

She rushes to the telephone, but the crashing plane has clipped the lines. With a strange airplane smoldering across the road and fire rapidly surrounding her house, Foster flees her home with Tiffany in her arms.

L.B. Barrett and his son, Randy, abandon their cattle in a nearby field and rush to the airplane. What they find is astonishingly surreal – the airplane, badly damaged and smoking angrily, is resting incongruently upright on its landing gear, the left engine running as though ready for take-off, minus wings and full of fire.

The pilot, his skin and clothes charred, falls from the left side cockpit window, picks himself up and runs away from the burning machine toward the Barrett's. Before they can speak he frantically barks orders: Call the fire department; there are more people trapped in the plane; we need ambulances; Life Flight. As they try to calm him, the co-pilot, hideously burned, appears like an apparition, walking toward them through the tall grass.

Donald Lewis rushes up on his John Deere and is greeted by the explosion of the airplane's overheated tires. Seconds later, Don Ruggles lands his private helicopter near the crash. He, too, has witnessed the horror, but from the air.

Oblivious to his injuries, the pilot provides his wife's phone number for Lewis with orders to call her immediately and let her know he is OK, then returns to sit with his horribly burned co-pilot on a slight hill nearby.

They watch, helpless and in agony, as fire screams like blowtorches from every opening in the fuselage. What they – and only they – know is, when firemen arrive, they will find inside the smoldering hull the remains of the man for whom the phrase "Teen Idol" was invented, along with his fiancé and every musician in his popular band: Rick Nelson and the Stone Canyon Band.

As they hear the first ambulance coming down the road, the pilot turns to his co-pilot with a final urgent order: Don't tell anyone about the heater.

Rick Nelson, Teen Idol

ERIC "RICKY" HILLIARD NELSON was named after his mother's side of the family. Oswald George "Ozzie" Nelson hired Harriet Hilliard in 1932 to sing in his orchestra. Three years later, they married. Their first child, David, was born in 1936 and Ricky followed in 1940. The family settled into their home in Tenafly, N.J., with Harriet exchanging singing for motherhood, but the demands of leading a popular dance band kept Ozzie on the road. So when he was offered a steady job as orchestra leader for Red Skelton's radio program, he took it even though it meant uprooting the family and moving to Hollywood.

Three years later, when Skelton left the radio program, the time slot was offered to Ozzie. He developed a program that centered on his real life family and called it, *The Adventures of Ozzie and Harriett.* His character was the just-slightly-out-of-step father figure to Harriett's reassuring wife. Actors played the parts of Dave, the quiet but earnest son, and Ricky, the smarty-pants. Eventually, the real life sons prevailed on Ozzie to let them play themselves and in February 1949, they made their debut.

The next year, ABC approached Ozzie with the idea of moving the popular radio show to a new fangled medium – television. However, Ozzie was not sure whether what worked in front of microphones would work in front of cameras. So, he tested the waters by producing a small budget film, *Here Comes the Nelsons.*

It was not a blockbuster, but it did well enough on the big screen to convince Ozzie that the Nelson family was ready for the small one. *The Adventures of Ozzie and Harriett* debuted on ABC-TV in fall 1952 and became television's first and longest running family sitcom. It also made the Nelsons American icons, the epitome of the wholesome, nuclear family.

Ricky was 12 years old when he became a national TV star and, by the time he reached high school two years later, he was making $100,000 a year.

It was an event in high school, he would later claim, that turned him to music. The story, perhaps apocryphal, is that Ricky had a crush on a high school sweetheart, but the feelings were not mutual. On what he figured would be their last date, she swooned when Elvis came on the radio, so Ricky claimed he, too, was about to make a record. Instead of being impressed, she laughed in his face. You, a record? Yeah, right.

To save face, Ricky turned to the one person he knew in the music business – Ozzie. Like a good father, Ozzie pulled a few of his considerable strings. Suddenly, Ricky had a deal to record three songs: *I'm Walking, A Teenager's Romance, and You're My One and Only Love.*

In a flash of promotional brilliance, it occurred to Ozzie that *The Adventures of Ozzie and Harriet* could be used to further Ricky's singing career. After all, a captive audience of millions tuned in every week.

On April 10, 1957, Ozzie allowed Ricky to sing, *I'm Walking* on *The Adventures of Ozzie and Harriett* and the song quickly rose to No. 17 on the charts. Then the B side, *A Teenager's Romance* hit and rose to No. 2. Suddenly, Ricky Nelson was not only a popular TV star, he was also the hottest young heartthrob in the record business.

Life Magazine put the handsome, blue-eyed teen's picture on the cover and coined a term to describe him: "Teen Idol." His high school sweetheart, would not be laughing now.

With his natural talents, careful song selection, and Ozzie's promotional largess – Ricky was allowed to perform a song at the end of almost every episode of *The Adventures of Ozzie and Harriett*, whether it had anything remotely to do with the plot or not. Ricky became the No. 2 selling singer of the day, right behind Elvis Presley.

Between 1957 and 1961, he wracked up more than two-dozen hits, including *A Teenager's Romance, Be Bop Baby, Stood up, Believe What You Say, Lonesome Town, Poor Little Fool, I Got a Feeling, Never Be Anyone Else But You, It's Late, Just a Little Too Much, Sweeter Than You, Young Emotions, Travelin' Man, Hello Mary Lou, A Wonder Like You* and *Everlovin'*.

Remarkably, he had all those hits without hitting the road. With his TV commitments, there was no time for the traditional touring. Besides, why tour? He would sing in your home once a week.

In 1959, at the height of his recording and TV popularity, he starred in the hit movie, *Rio Bravo*, and a year later in *The Wackiest Ship in the Navy*. At the age of 20, Ricky Nelson was a star of radio, television, movies and records.

On his 21st birthday, he dropped the "y" to mark his coming of age, and the next year "Rick" crowned his achievements by signing a then unheard of 20-year, million-dollar contract with Decca Records. It was the pinnacle of his success and the beginning of his decline.

Within months, The Beatles arrived and Nelson, the Everly Brothers, Eddie Cochran and all the other American Pop singers were rendered passé by the British Invasion. The title of his first release for Decca, *You Don't Love Me Anymore* said it all. The song never made the Top 40.

At least one person still loved Rick – Kristen Harmon, daughter of football star Tom Harmon. Rick and Kristen married in April 1963. Six months later, Kristen gave birth to their first of four children, daughter Tracy Kristine Nelson.

With his recording career in decline, Rick suffered another professional blow in 1966. ABC cancelled *The Adventures of Ozzie and Harriett*. However, it was a thrown-in-the-briar-patch setback. Free of the rigorous television rehearsal schedule, Rick could finally do what he had dreamed of doing all along – touring.

He was still popular in Asia and enjoyed a successful tour of much of the Far East. When he returned, he was forced to fill his schedule with bit parts on television. He even tried his hand performing in a musical comedy.

It might not have appeared so to the casual observer, but it was an intensely creative time for Rick.

He had become increasingly interested in a new type of music, a smooth blend of both Country and Pop. He assembled some of the best sidemen in the business and began recording songs by the country's top songwriters. He even scored a minor Country-Rock hit with his friend Bob Dylan, *She Belongs to Me*, in 1970.

In a bitterly ironic reversal of opinions, the critics who earlier dismissed "Ricky" as simply a pretty boy with the good fortune to be born of a show biz father were won over by his new style, while fans of Ricky's earlier music now abandoned him, sometimes angrily.

It was one thing to be aware of declining records sales, but quite another for Rick to come face to face with the animosity of fans who felt he had betrayed them, personally and musically, simply by growing up. It happened in October 1971 during a "Rock 'n Roll Revival" concert at Madison Square Garden. The audience came to see a musical time warp – performers from the 1950s and 1960s still doing their acts in the 1970s.

They were all there – Chuck Berry, Bo Diddley and Bobby Rydell. And they stuck to the format, except for Rick.

With shoulder length hair, purple shirt and bell-bottom jeans, he no longer resembled that "nice young boy on TV." The booing began almost immediately, even when he sang some early hits. By the time he sang his version of the Rolling Stones' *Honky Tonk Women* the audience was in full rebellion.

Like Dylan playing electric at the Newport Folk Festival six years earlier, the audience booed Rick from the stage. It was a galvanizing experience and from it came his personal anthem, the song *Garden Party*.

Garden Party, an ode to life without compromise, was released in 1972 and became Rick's first million-selling hit since 1961. It was also his last.

For the next 13 years, Rick's career languished. The Stone Canyon Band broke up and so did his marriage to Kristen, who took their four children when she left.

His work was limited to playing bit parts on television and making guest appearances on variety shows.

Then in 1985, Rick performed on a Rock 'n Roll Nostalgia Tour of England. It went surprisingly well and revived some interest in his dormant singing career. He returned to the states determined to capitalize on it. He put together a new Stone Canyon Band and booked a tour.

Once again, it was time "to be somewhere tomorrow, to smile and do my show."

By Dec. 31, 1985, Rick Nelson and his reconstituted Stone Canyon Band have been traveling the southern United States on a multi-stop series of performances, the last of which would be a New Year's Eve show in Dallas.

However, at the moment, they are sitting in their cold, 41-year-old former military cargo plane on the tarmac at the Guntersville, Ala., airport going nowhere. Looking through the window, the left engine's propeller rotates through several cycles but refuses to light. Eventually, fuel pours from the engine case drain line, and the pilot gives up and tries the right engine. Thankfully, it fires right up. But when he tries the reluctant left engine again, it simply will not start.

Rick, his fiancé Helen Blair, 29, and the members of the Stone Canyon Band – Andy Chapin, 30, Rick Intveld, 23, Bobby Neal, 38, Clark Russell, 35, and Patrick Woodward, 35 – have had enough of sitting in a cold tin can waiting for an engine that will not crank. They open the rear door and make the cold walk back into the terminal, leaving the pilots to trouble shoot the engine.

Undoubtedly, when the pilots discover the cause it will not be as exotic as the problem at the previous night's concert in Guntersville. During the performance, Rick noticed a peculiar odor on stage. As it grew worse, he realized it was coming from his small guitar amplifier, a putrid smell. After the concert, he checked the amplifier and discovered a boa constrictor coiled among the hot electrical components. He removed the snake, but the smell was there to stay.

The pilot, Brad Rank, who also doubles as the plane's mechanic, comes into the passenger lounge with good news and bad news. He has fixed the engine – just a clogged engine primer line he has blown out with compressed air. However, in the time it has taken to fix the engine, the weather has turned worse. Rick and the band will have to wait for it to improve. Rank is not going to fly in bad weather, not in a DC-3.

THE DOUGLAS DC-3 is, perhaps, the most accomplished airplane ever built. It first flew on Dec. 17, 1935, exactly 32 years after Wilbur and Orville flew at Kitty Hawk. It is the first true "airliner." American Airlines used it for the New York to Chicago route, and it became the first airplane to make a profit solely by transporting passengers. Other airlines ordered DC-3s as fast as Douglas could make them and, by 1939, 90 percent of the world's passengers were being flown on DC-3s.

Nearly 11,000 of them were built in the United States and about 2,500 more by companies licensed in Japan and the Soviet Union. It could carry between 21 and 28 passengers, but since it was not pressurized, it could not carry them very high. For its time though, it could move them reasonably fast. The two radial engines cranked out 1,200 horsepower each, enough to push the DC-3 along at cruising speeds in excess of 200 mph. More importantly, it could carry passengers farther, non-stop, than other transports of the day.

When World War II broke out, the American military needed a cargo plane that could carry a heavy load a long way. With extra tanks added, the DC-3 fit the bill. The Army Air Force pressed thousands into service giving it the military designation of C-47. President Dwight Eisenhower later praised the C-47/DC-3 as the single most important aircraft in the Allied War effort. After the war, thousands of C-47s were surplus and made their way back into civilian service.

Such was the case of Rick's airplane, N711Y. It began life as part of the war effort in 1944 – C-47 serial 13650. In 1959, it was converted from a C-47 to a DC-3 and refurbished with an "executive" interior – two triple seat divans facing each other in the front of the cabin, four single seats in the middle, and two double seat couches facing each other in the rear.

BY 12:40 P.M., BOTH THE WEATHER and the engines seem more cooperative and the band boards the DC-3 once again. Rick and Helen settle into what has become their customary place on the couches in the rear, the rest of the band scatter throughout the cabin. This time both engines fire up easily. Now if the balky passenger compartment heater will work as well, this flight might be OK after all.

The passenger compartment's gasoline heater has been the object of damnation and consternation for everyone on board. The co-pilot is scared to death of it because he does not like combustion anywhere on an airplane outside the engine. Everyone else hates it because it so rarely works.

It had become such an issue that two months earlier, Pilot Rank had flown the DC-3 to a shop in Lincoln, Neb., just to have the heater examined. The mechanics checked and serviced it and it worked well, at least for a while. However, it does not today. Once the airplane climbs up into the frigid December air, the cold soaked airplane gets even colder, and that is when the temperamental gasoline heater begins to "act up." What happened next depends on who tells the tale.

Co-pilot Kenneth Ferguson remembers the heater's "over-heat" warning light illuminating in the instrument panel. So, the crew turns off the heater with a control switch in the cockpit, wait a while and turn it back on only to have the "over-heat" warning illuminate again.

After going through this sequence several times, Ferguson says, "(Pilot) Brad (Rank) decided to go aft in the tail (where the heater box is located) to see if there was anything he could do to get it to function correctly … there were several times involved here… he signaled me to turn it on or he came up to the front and told me to turn it on… this happened several times." Each time co-pilot Ferguson becomes more convinced the problematic little heater should be left alone. Finally, he has enough.

"I refused to turn it on. I didn't turn it on. I was getting nervous. I didn't think we should be messing with that heater en route. I had discussed this with Brad on previous flights and he said, 'Rick wants heat,' and he turned it on again." Once again, the "over-heat" light illuminates and the heater is turned off and later on again. Then, with Pilot Rank in the tail checking the heater, band member Patrick Woodward comes into the cockpit with news that shoots adrenaline to the heart: "We've got smoke back here in the cabin."

Rank, on the other hand, remembers leaving the cockpit late in the flight to check on the passengers. Rick and Helen are asleep on the couches in the rear; the others are resting variously around the cabin. As he stops at mid-cabin to make small talk with Patrick Woodward, Rank sees smoke coming from beneath the couches where Rick and Helen are sleeping. He goes immediately to the rear of the plane, through a closet to the narrow baggage area, and pretzels through an access door to the rear fuselage where the heater is located. He finds no smoke nor fire and the heater is cold to the touch.

Still, just to be safe, he sets off one of the two fire extinguishers permanently affixed to the heater.

He squeezes back toward the cabin, but, as he squirms through the baggage area, he lifts the plane's cloth prop covers that are covering Rick's smelly amplifier and suddenly clouds of thick smoke billow up in his face. He drops the covers and hurries back through to the cabin where Rick and Helen awake with a start.

An alarming amount of smoke has filled the cabin, and the seepage beneath the couches has spread to every crevice all the way to the front of the passenger compartment. Coming down the aisle, Woodward confronts Rank, "What are we going to do?" Rank orders the passengers to open all the fresh air vents; he is going to the cockpit to land the airplane – now.

As Rank reaches the cockpit, Ferguson is already sounding the alarm to air traffic control.

"Fort Worth, Douglas seven eleven yankee."

"Douglas seven one one yankee, go ahead."

"I think I'd like to turn around and head for Texarkana here, I've got a little problem."

"Yeah, Douglas, uh, seven one one Yankee, uh roger, cleared to Texarkana airport via direct and advise of any assistance you need."

"Give us vectors for starters. Texarkana's the closest decent airport there, is that affirmative?"

"Uh seven one one yankee, uh, that's the closest, uh, fairly good sized airport, uh, seven one one yankee, need heading of, uh, zero nine zero degrees for, uh, Texarkana."

"Zero nine zero."

Co-pilot Ferguson initiates a turn to the east, toward the Texarkana airport. As Pilot Rank slides into the seat next to him and takes over the controls, the smoke grows so dense neither pilot can see the other.

Suddenly, Texarkana is not an option. The plane must land immediately. Rank quickly puts the lumbering plane into an emergency dive and looks for anywhere to land the burning airplane.

"Uh, Ft. Worth, just any field will do, we've got a problem here."

"OK, one one yankee, can you make it back to Texarkana?"

"Negative, we've got to get on the ground."

Before the air traffic controller can respond, helicopter pilot Don Ruggles, flying nearby and listening to the drama unfold interrupts him.

"Ft. Worth Center, this is helicopter …"

But the air traffic controller is frantically searching his charts for a landing strip and has no time for the helicopter pilot.

"OK, helicopter, standby just a second …one one yankee, I've got Red River County Airport that's back at your, uh, 6 o'clock position now and 19 miles, uh that would be the nearest airport to you. Mount Pleasant is south of you off at, uh, about 160 degrees heading and 22 miles if you want to attempt Mount Pleasant."

Nineteen miles or 22 miles, either might as well be a million. The pilots and passengers are gagging and blinded by the dense, acrid smoke. And it is getting worse, much worse.

This plane must land now.

The roiling, black smoke stains the instruments and fogs the cockpit windows. Gasping, Ferguson does his best to let someone know.

"We've smoke in the cockpit."

"One one yankee, you're breaking up, uh, can you state the nature of your emergency?"

An Eagle Express pilot has heard what the controller has not and relays the emergency.

"Said he had smoke in the cockpit, Center, seventeen fifty six is relaying."

"Eagle Express seventeen fifty six, thank you and Eagle Express seventeen fifty six, ask him if he can make it to Mount Pleasant."

"Douglas seven eleven yankee, can you make it to Mount

Pleasant?"

But there is no hope of finding Mount Pleasant. Desperate for air, the pilots have opened the cockpit windows and their navigational charts have been sucked out.

"Seven one yankee...we don't know where it is. We've lost our charts."

"Right on your tail and 17 miles."

"Can't do it."

Gagging and unable to see, Rank's only hope is to stretch out the cockpit's side window and fly the plane with one hand on the control yoke, fire burning his body and wind battering his face. Ferguson unbuckles his belt and squirms to avoid the flames growing from the floor around him, but the open window sucks even more smoke and fire into the cockpit. Rank calls out for Ferguson to lower the gear and flaps and Ferguson forces his hands into the fire that engulfs the control handles to his left.

As his flesh burns, he pulls the levers and deploys both the landing gear and flaps. With his hands too badly burned to re-buckle his seat belt, he places his back and head against the instrument panel and windshield and braces for the crash.

The pilots of both the Eagle Express airliner and the helicopter turn toward the burning DC-3 in flat out sprints to intercept it and offer whatever help they can.

Rank, his head out the window, squints through the battering wind and spots a field. Unable to see the airplane's instruments, he uses instinct and "feel" to roll left and set up an approach.

Farmer Barrett and his son drop their work as they see the smoking DC-3 bearing down on a nearby field. Atop his John Deere a few fields away, Lewis sees it, too, an airplane burning, literally melting, dripping molten aluminum, setting on fire the fields over which it is passing. Schoolteacher Foster gasps as the plane cuts through two telephone poles and crash-lands in the field across the road.

Helicopter pilot Don Ruggles, having been put on hold by the air traffic controller, tries the Eagle Express pilot.

"Seventeen fifty six, you copy the helicopter."

"Affirmative, go ahead."

"Uh, we have the aircraft in sight. Looks like he's gone down. You need to call Texarkana for the Air Life helicopter. "

Ruggles lands his helicopter as the Eagle Express pilot orbits nearby, relaying details back to the Air Traffic controller in Ft Worth. A number of residents and even police have seen the burning DC-3 on its final approach to the field and flood the local 911 center with calls.

Fire trucks and ambulances scramble out of Texarkana. The Air Life medi-vac helicopter arrives from Fort Worth. Firemen with the Texarkana airport's crash/rescue fire truck arrive and pump 1,000 gallons of water and 500 pounds of dry powder onto the plane. They eventually extinguish the fire. Pilot Brad Rank is evacuated by ambulance, co-pilot Ferguson by helicopter. Deputies from the Bowie County Sheriff's department set up a perimeter and secure the airplane from sightseers and reporters. There is nothing left to do now but wait for it to cool.

UNDER THE GLARE of portable lights, emergency workers enter the burned out hull at 2:30 a.m. Jan. 1, 1986. Five members of the Bowie County Sheriff's Department, an investigator from the NTSB and two members of a local funeral home pick through the ashes and discover the remains of Rick, his fiancé and band. The bodies are tagged and carefully removed. The job is finished before the New Year is four hours old.

ALTHOUGH NEW YEAR'S DAY 1986, was a federal holiday, an NTSB investigation was already ramping up. Still, it would take months to determine why the DC-3 fell burning from the Texas sky. There were several false leads, the first coming even before the fire was out. Agents from U.S. Customs had been tracking an airplane out of Mexico but lost it over Louisiana. The Federal agents called the Bowie County Sheriff's Office and warned this could be their plane. They urged the deputies to "watch out for anything suspicious."

Some members of the media developed theories of their own. Upon learning hairspray cans were found in the wreckage, some speculated the fire was started by band members using the canisters as torches to freebase cocaine. It apparently did not occur to them that a band of longhaired musicians might simply use hairspray as, well... hairspray.

NTSB investigators quickly zeroed in on the problematic gasoline heater. And for good reason. Even though the pilots gave considerably differing versions of the final flight, both verified a problem with the gasoline heater. Then, of course, there was the heater's troubled history, verified both by the pilots and by documents recovered from the shop that had serviced it.

But there was a problem, too, with the "heater-caused-the-fire" theory. In sworn testimony, Capt. Rank said he checked the heater after seeing smoke rising from the beneath the couch in the rear of the airplane. He testified the heater was cold when he touched it. Still, to be safe, he says, he activated the fire extinguisher that is built into the heater. How could a gasoline heater burning out of control be cold to the touch? And even if it was on fire, surely activating its built-in fire extinguisher would stop it right then and there wouldn't it? Instead, the fire worsened after he says the extinguisher was activated.

After months of exhaustive investigation, the NTSB conclusion was obvious to the most casual observer: "*The National Transportation Safety Board determines that the Probable Cause of this accident is 'Fuselage/Cabin Fire,'*" but the NTSB stopped short of naming the source of the fire, writing only that it was "*undetermined.*" The board also noted that Capt. Rank failed to follow proper emergency procedures when he 1) opened the windows and vents; 2) failed to used the on-board oxygen masks; 3) failed to combat the fire with the plane's hand-held fire extinguishers.

Apparently, they gave him no bonus points for masterfully landing a burning airplane with his head out the window and flames at his feet.

RICK NELSON WAS BURIED in Forest Lawn Cemetery in Los Angeles, survived by a daughter and three sons. Many mourned his death much like the passing of a family friend; after all, we'd grown up with Ricky. He was the kid down the block that came to visit once a week; he set the standard for what every pubescent boy and girl of the era wanted: to either be, or date, a Teen Idol. Then he grew up to become the local boy who did well, earning the respect of his industry and doing it on his own terms.

Rick Nelson was posthumously inducted into the Rock and Roll Hall of Fame and the Rockabilly Hall of Fame.

His high school sweetheart, if she ever really existed, would have been impressed.

Oddities and Ironies

RICK NELSON'S 1961 VIDEO of *Travelin' Man* is considered by many to be the world's first music video.

Bob Dylan was on tour when Rick died. At his next several concerts, he stopped his show and talked with the audience about his friendship with Rick before playing *Lonesome Town*.

Rick Nelson's daughter, Tracy, became a movie and television star while his twin sons, Mathew and Gunnar, became Pop stars in their own right. Youngest son Sam is a Hard Rock musician.

As America's first "TV Mom," Harriet Hilliard Nelson raised her children and lived her family life in the living rooms of America. She learned of Rick's death in her own living room while watching television.

Dad Ozzie had succumbed to cancer in 1975.

THE WRITING'S ON THE WALL...

Stevie Ray Vaughan

Died: Aug. 27, 1990, Alpine Valley Resort, East Troy, Wis.

GUITAR LEGEND ERIC CLAPTON opens his dressing room door to better hear the music. On stage, just a short walk away, a blues guitarist is blistering his 1959 Stratocaster and working the Blues like few ever have. Listening intently, Clapton marvels at the passion and perfection. He steps across the room and turns on a video monitor to watch the performance.

Beneath a flat-brimmed bandito hat, the guitarist grimaces as he strikes a soulful note, bends it, stretches it, and holds it without mercy, sustaining the note to the breaking point. Without warning, he releases it and rips through an impossible riff – his hand gliding across the oversized neck, molding the music, burnishing the notes, punching the accents with the Holy Ghost passion of a Primitive Baptist preacher.

The spirit moves the crowd and some jump to their feet, shouting, arms raised in victory. Others simply stare, transfixed in the rare and cathartic moment – the revelation of truth, the expression of life – pain, heartbreak, redemption, and joy – the arc of his own life defined with commitment so total and skill so perfect the performer and performance are one.

Watching the monitor, Clapton feels diminished and wonders if he will ever get to that level of commitment, that point to which this master rises?

Later that night, at the end of his own performance, Clapton invites the guitarist on stage to join him for an encore. Clapton introduces him as "one of the greatest guitar players in the world." Along with guitar legends Buddy Guy, Jimmy Vaughan and Robert Cray, they play a white hot, 20-minute, guitar-dueling version of the blues classic *Sweet Home Chicago* that leaves them and the audience exhilarated and exhausted.

Afterward, in the last available seat of a helicopter hired to shuttle the musicians and crew from the outdoor amphitheater back to Chicago, guitarist Stevie Ray Vaughan relaxes. He has survived his demons and conquered the music industry finally, to reclaim his rightful place among "the best guitar players in the world."

The next morning on a foggy hillside, rescue workers will find his body amid the wreckage.

Stevie Ray Vaughan

HE WAS NOT BORN WITH A GUITAR IN HIS HAND, but it did not take long. When he turned seven in 1961, Stevie Ray Vaughan got his first guitar – a toy "Western" guitar from Sears. His 10-year-old brother, Jimmy, was already playing guitar and would later gain fame in his own right with his band The Fabulous Thunderbirds. Stevie, inspired by the fun Jimmy was having, devoted himself to his plastic instrument.

During the next couple of years, both brothers' skill advanced quickly. Jimmy took mercy on Stevie and his little plastic guitar, giving him a hand-me-down Gibson. Stevie was now a "real" guitar player – or at least now he played a real guitar.

Jimmy tutored Stevie in the rudiments, but more importantly, he taught Stevie to teach himself. Stevie spent endless hours by the record player listening to Albert Collins, B.B. King, Howlin Wolf, T-Bone Walker, Jimi Hendrix and others. He later admitted he played his first record, Lonnie Mack's *Wham*, so frequently his annoyed father finally broke it.

He listened, absorbed, and then practiced endless hours to recreate the music of the masters.

By their teens, both Stevie and Jimmy were playing regularly with various bands in their hometown of Dallas. However, their parents, Jim, an asbestos plant worker, and Martha, a cement factory secretary and devout Christian, were becoming increasingly concerned that the boy's, late hours in local bars could lead to the wayward life of alcohol and drugs.

Rather than endure the lectures, Jimmy moved out and planted his stake in the fertile musical soil of Austin, leaving 13-year-old Stevie behind to live with their parents admonitions.

Three years later, while working in a Dallas fast food restaurant, Stevie had an epiphany that led him to do the same. During a later television interview, he would describe "The Grease Incident."

"Part of my job was to clean out the trash bins. One night, I was standing on top of a barrel, the top caved in. I fell in grease up to (my chest), and right then I decided 'I'm not gonna do this anymore. I'm gonna play guitar,'" Stevie recalled.

At the age of 17, Stevie quit high school and moved to Austin, too. He spent the early 1970s playing in various bands with varying degrees of success. He left his first band, Krackerjack, when the leader insisted the musicians wear makeup, then joined Marc Benno's band and recorded an album for A&M Records, but the album was never released.

Eventually, he joined a popular Austin band, The Cobras, and played five nights a week for more than two years. In spring 1977, an Austin Music poll voted The Cobras Band of the Year. Despite their success, Stevie left The Cobras later in the year and formed a new R&B band with Lou Ann Barton, Mike Kindred, W.C. Clark, Freddie Pharaoh and Johnny Reno.

Stevie had begun hanging out at Alexander's, a gas station, barbecue and beer place just outside Austin. He would sit in with the bands, fitting in as needed – one night playing guitar, the next singing and the next playing drums. Because of his multiple talents, the locals began calling him Triple Threat. So, when it came time to pick a name for his new band, it seemed obvious: He called it The Triple Threat Revue. It was the precursor to the band that would accompany him to fame.

The Triple Threat Revue stayed together until 1980. By then Stevie had decided the band had too many leaders. So, he and Lou Ann Barton spun off to form yet another band.

Again, the name seemed obvious – the two of them having been the "trouble-makers" from The Triple Threat Review. They would call this new band Double Trouble. The added bonus - Double Trouble was also the title of a favorite song by Otis Rush.

Consequently, Double Trouble had double implications.

Double Trouble evolved through several personnel changes. When Lou Ann left, Stevie took on the additional role of singer. Eventually, he settled on two musicians from his past as permanent sidemen – Tommy Shannon and Chris Layton.

Tommy, the former bassist for Johnny Winter, remembers having first met Stevie at a club called The Fog in Dallas where Stevie, although only in his early teens, was playing. Tommy recognized the "scrawny little kid" had a gift for music and introduced himself. Later, Stevie recalled how the older musicians shunned him because of his youth, but Tommy was one of the few who did not treat him like a pest.

Chris had first come to Stevie's attention back during The Cobras' years. However, Chris had actually discovered Stevie first. Passing by the Soap Creek Saloon in Austin one night, Chris was drawn inside by a piercing guitar. He was astonished to find a skinny young kid playing "unbelievable" guitar. Chris left, hoping to get an opportunity to play with this remarkable young guitar player.

The opportunity happened shortly afterward when The Cobras' drummer, exhausted from working his day job as a construction worker, over-slept for a gig. The Cobra's sax player, Joe Sublet, quickly called his to fill in. It was Chris Layton.

Long before the days of helicopters and private jets, Stevie, Chris and Tommy toured gig-to-gig in an old milk truck they called "The African Queen." It had a couch behind the front seats, and their gear was piled in behind that. They had rigged a bed above it all where they would crawl up and get some sleep, at least until the driver hit the brakes, and then the whole thing would slide forward. They were not making much money, but they loved what they were doing and the fans loved them, too. Double Trouble quickly became fixtures on the Texas music scene.

In 1981, they played a benefit organized by fellow Texan Joe Ely, and after seeing a videotape of the performance, Mick Jagger invited Double Trouble to play for a private party at the Danceteria in New York City. That performance on April 22,

1982, lead to Double Trouble's big break – a performance that summer at the prestigious Montreaux International Jazz Festival.

Double Trouble was the first band without a record deal to be asked to the festival, and after their performance some purists might have wondered if it was a mistake to have invited them. The stage was designed for acoustic jazz, but Stevie, Chris and Tommy came in with big Fender amplifiers. Even after turning them down, Double Trouble was still loud by comparison.

A few booed, but only a few. Most were stunned by this unknown trio and after the show they gathered with guests in the "musicians lounge" where they drank and enjoyed the praise of music industry luminaries, including Rock star David Bowie.

With no performance scheduled the next day, Double Trouble's manager booked them – without pay – to play in the musician's lounge while Jackson Brown performed on the main stage.

Afterward, Brown and his band repaired to the lounge and joined Double Trouble in a jam session that lasted until well after daybreak.

On the strength of their Montreaux appearance Stevie received two offers: David Bowie offered Stevie a job playing guitar on his upcoming album, and Jackson Brown offered Double Trouble a week's worth of free studio time at his Los Angeles recording studio. Stevie accepted both offers.

Suddenly, Stevie's career was moving quickly. In late 1982, he spent three days with Bowie recording the guitar tracks for what would become Bowie's *Let's Dance* album; then Stevie and Double Trouble spent three days at Brown's "Downtown" recording studio in Los Angeles cutting what they intended to be demo tracks for their own album.

To help trim expenses, Brown gave the group used audio tape to record over – the same tape he had used for his *Lawyers in*

Love album. Legendary A&R man John Hammond, Sr., landed Stevie and Double Trouble a record deal with Epic Records.

Bowies' *Let's Dance* album was a hit. He mounted a world tour to coincide with the album's release and invited Stevie to go along as lead guitar. But Stevie felt his future lay with Double Trouble, not David Bowie. So, to Bowie's chagrin and everyone's amazement, Stevie turned down the offer to play with one of Rock's great stars and put all his chips on Double Trouble.

The demo tracks Double Trouble recorded at Brown's Los Angeles studio were so impressive that on June 13, 1983, Epic released it as *Texas Flood* – Stevie and Double Trouble's first album.

It shook the music world. *Texas Flood* was nominated for two Grammy's, and Stevie won three Guitar Player Magazine's Reader Polls: Best New Talent; Best Blues Album; and Best Electric Guitarist, which he won every year until 1991. *Texas Flood* finally reached No. 38 on the charts and re-ignited a worldwide interest in the Blues.

Stevie and Double Trouble capitalized on their sudden success with non-stop touring. Finally, they could afford to retire The African Queen milk truck.

They were rapidly building a national fan base and more fans were on the way with the release in May 1984 of their second album, *Couldn't Stand the Weather.*

It was even more successful than their first, reaching No. 31 on the charts, and turned Stevie and Double Trouble into bona fide headliners. It also meant continuing what had become a wearying succession of one-night stands, but now in increasingly larger halls.

Looking to broaden their sound, Stevie added keyboardist Reese Wynans to Double Trouble in 1985, and released the bands third album, *Soul to Soul.* It, too, was wildly successful.

Three hit albums, critical acclaim and headliner status. By 1985, Stevie had developed the Midas touch, but like Midas, he was about to pay a terrible price. Beneath the fame and fortune, his parent's fears were being fully realized. Both Stevie and bassist Tommy had fully embraced the "Rock 'n Roll lifestyle" of endless partying and constant drug abuse.

By the time the band recorded *Soul to Soul*, Stevie's addictions had become so serious that even though the recording was made in his hometown, Stevie stayed in a hotel, rather than his parents' house, to avoid discovery.

Aggravating matters, by 1986 Stevie Ray Vaughan and Double Trouble was not just a great Blues band; it was a huge business with huge bills – a great lumbering machine with its own momentum. The band replaced manager Chelsey Milliken with Alex Hodges and hoped Hodges would slow the machine.

Instead, after reviewing the books, Hodges determined they would have to keep up the frenetic schedule just to pay the rent.

A world tour and plans for a live album increased the pressure. Now, the drugs and alcohol that initially lubricated the machine, ground the gears.

Finally, one night in a Dallas hotel, desperately ill from drug abuse and with nowhere to turn, Stevie and Tommy knelt and earnestly prayed for God to deliver them. They wept from their hearts until they could weep no more. Exhausted, they composed themselves, then snorted another line of coke and opened another bottle of booze.

On Aug. 27, 1986, "Big Jim" Vaughan, Stevie's dad, died unexpectedly. The band immediately broke off their tour and returned home for the funeral. Some hoped the tragedy surely would serve to turn off the machine for at least a short break. But within hours of burying his father, Stevie and Double

Trouble were on a jet bound for a show that night in Montreal.

Stevie insisted the machine keep turning, telling the others that playing was the only way he knew to cope, and he would deal with the consequences later. It would only take a month.

On a tour stop in the small town of Ludwigshafen, Germany, Stevie and Chris were on the street in the early morning hours when Stevie fell abruptly to his knees confused, and retching blood, mumbling insistently that he needed a drink. But with the bars closed, there was nothing to drink and no drugs available. He regained himself long enough to make it back to the hotel and collapsed on the bed – ashen, shaking and sweating.

Chris hurried to call for an ambulance as Stevie's eyes, fixed on the ceiling, went lifeless. Chris hung up and looked into Stevie's dark, empty eyes and saw ... nothing, like the eyes of a dead animal.

The horror grew over long moments as Stevie's lifeless body lay still on the hotel bed. Then, dimly at first, a flicker of life returned to his eyes and slowly Stevie came back from somewhere very far away. He sat up carefully, looked around the room and said quietly, "I need help."

Stevie struggled through two more shows, then turned off the machine. He cancelled the remaining 21 concerts on the tour and checked into a London hospital. Shortly afterwards, he returned to the United States and on Oct. 13, 1986, Stevie entered a rehabilitation facility in Atlanta. On the same day, Tommy entered a similar facility in Austin. This time their commitment to sobriety was so profound it even inspired two members of the crew to become clean and sober.

While Stevie and Tommy concentrated on regaining their health, Chris and Reese worked to piece together a double "live" album. It was released as *Live Alive* in November 1986.

Now sober, Stevie spent much of the next year lying low and re-evaluating his life. He would look back on his addiction and say, "I don't drink or get high because I have all these problems; I have these problems because I drink and get high. I realize now that nothing's so bad that getting drunk or getting high is gonna make it better."

He rigorously adhered to the Alcoholics Anonymous 12-Step Program and wrote a collection of songs – musical confessions – that chronicled his struggle. He and Double Trouble entered the studio sober for the first time, and wondered whether the magic would be there when the drugs were not. With clear heads and newfound spirituality, their playing was more disciplined and their approach more practical. The songs became the album *In Step* – a reference to the 12-Step Program that now guided their lives. Released in 1989, it won a Grammy for Best Contemporary Blues Record. Some hailed it as Stevie's finest effort.

And there was a labor of love on his agenda. For years Stevie and Jimmy Vaughan had wanted to do a "brothers" album, but with Stevie's relentless touring and Jimmy's work with The Fabulous Thunderbirds, there had been scant time for the indulgence. Now that Stevie had slowed the machine, the brothers booked Ardent Studio's in Memphis in spring 1990, and finally recorded the tracks. They had come a long way since their parent's living room and Stevie's plastic guitar.

With the brothers' album in the can and now sober, rested, and healthy, Stevie and Double Trouble headed out on tour co-headlining with Jeff Beck and Joe Cocker. They played to full houses and enthusiastic crowds throughout early summer 1990.

One concert in particular awaited Stevie on the tour. A "Guitar Legends" concert which would feature his musical hero's – Eric Clapton, Robert Cray and Buddy Guy. Making it even more special, Stevie's brother, Jimmy, was scheduled to sit in with Double Trouble during their part of the show. It was a two-night stand set for the small ski resort of Alpine Valley, near Elkhorn, Wis., about 50 miles from Chicago, on Aug. 25 and Aug. 26, 1990.

AT THE END OF HIS PORTION of the concert at 11:55 p.m. Aug. 26, Clapton steps to the microphone and announces over the deafening roar of a sea of fans, "I'd like to bring out, to join me … ah … in truth, the best guitar players in the entire world, man. Buddy Guy, Stevie Ray Vaughan, Robert Cray and Jimmy Vaughan."

The crowd thunders as the guitarists stroll on stage, plug in their guitars and launch in to the blues classic, *Sweet Home Chicago*. It is a superstar summit – five icons playing a feverish, white-hot, guitar jam.

When it is Stevie's turn to solo, he strikes a note that cuts through bigger than the entire band and bends it beyond logic, then plays with the inspiration of a man possessed.

In the dark, on a golf course behind the outdoor amphitheater, sit four empty helicopters, their pilots, oblivious to the guitar heroics on stage, huddle nearby. When the concert ends it will be their job to load the musicians into the choppers and fly them back to Chicago. But there is a problem – the temperature is dropping and fog is developing on the slopes around the Alpine Valley Ski Resort – a particularly treacherous problem for pilots trying to see their way climbing through rising terrain.

But pilot Michael Cheek has brought relieving news. He has just landed after a round-trip to Chicago and tells the other pilots that despite the patchy ground fog in the area, "the weather was good." That issue settled, the pilots agree when it's time to leave, Cheek's helicopter will take off first, followed by pilot Phillip

Huth, then Jeff Brown, with pilot Robert Kenney being last.

The performers finish their high-energy encore and leave thousands screaming for more as they take their bows and wave good-bye. Double Trouble bassist Chris has watched the encore from the wings and meets Stevie backstage at 12:15 a.m. As they wait for the amphitheater to clear out, they wind down with the kind of chat between friends that's simultaneously about everything and nothing at all. After about 30 minutes, Stevie excuses himself and says he's got to go back to the dressing room and get ready to leave, there's a pilot and helicopter waiting to fly him back to Chicago.

THE BELL 206B IS PERHAPS the most accomplished and the most popular helicopter ever built. Originally designed for the military, it has flown more hours and set or broken more records than any other single engine aircraft in the world. It is simply the most successful commercial helicopter and, with the best safety record of any single engine helicopter, it sets the standard for safety and reliability. A slightly altered version is used to train U.S. Army and U.S. Navy helicopter pilots.

PILOT JEFFERY WILLIAM BROWN, 48, is a veteran helicopter pilot. Not only is he a commercially rated pilot, he is also rated by the FAA as a helicopter instructor pilot. During the years, he has accrued more than 4,760 hours in flight and more than 1,500 of those are in the Bell 206B. He is also experienced in flying at night with more than 580 hours of flight time after the sun has gone down.

In addition to his experience in helicopters, Brown is also rated to fly single engine airplanes solely by reference to the aircraft's instruments, a vital skill when flying in clouds – or fog.

However, his instrument rating is specifically for airplanes. He does not have an instrument rating for helicopters.

ON THEIR WAY TO THE HELICOPTER at 12:55 a.m., Stevie, his brother Jimmy, and Jimmy's wife, Connie, stop and speak, again, with Chris. Stevie says he is eager to return to Chicago and call his girlfriend. He tells Chris to call him when he gets back home then starts to leave.

But after a few steps Stevie stops, turns back to Chris as though he remembers something, and says, "I love ya." He gives Chris a wink and disappears into the night.

AT THE LANDING ZONE there is another problem. Dew is settling on the helicopters, coating the windshields and making it impossible to see. As Stevie, Jimmy, and Connie approach chopper No. 3, a security guard is wiping the windshields with his shirt. They are surprised to find there is only one seat available in the helicopter, not the three they had been told to expect. The other seats have been taken by Bobby Brooks, Clapton's agent at Creative Artists Agency; Nigel Browne, a Clapton bodyguard; and Colin Smythe, one of Clapton's tour managers.

Exhausted and eager to get back to his hotel in Chicago, Stevie asks Jimmy and Connie if they mind if he takes the last seat. He explains as he climbs into the helicopter, "I really need to get back."

Dick Gomez finishes closing down the box office and joins his son and a friend as they walk across the emptying parking lot toward their car. In the background the noise of the stagehands banging and clanking as they disassembled the stage blends with the engines of the helicopters starting up.

At 1 a.m., Mike Cheek increases the power of helicopter No.

1 and it teeters into the air. As he climbs out, he radios the others that he has cleared the landing zone. Phillip Huth, piloting helicopter No. 2, powers up, climbs out and also calls "clear." Stevie and the three members of Clapton's entourage are strapped into helicopter No. 3 as pilot Jeff Brown powers up, climbs and radios that he, too, has cleared the landing zone. In helicopter No. 4, Clapton's manager Roger Forrester, is worried the fog has become too dense to fly safely. But pilot Robert Kenney reassures him it is only ground fog and as they lift off, Forrester is relieved to see it dissipate. He catches a quick glimpse of the lights from chopper No. 3 in front of them, but the lights veer quickly to the right and disappear.

Gomez, his son and friend stop to watch the lights as they thunder overhead and into the night. They see one set suddenly vanish. A moment later they hear a sharp metallic bang and rumble. Probably just the stage crew dropping something.

Joseph Cullivane does not think so. He and his niece had enjoyed the concert from the balcony of a room at the Alpine Ski Resort, then waited to watch the helicopters leave. They, too, see the lights of helicopter No. 3 disappear and hear a "thud." Fearing the worst, Cullivane grabs the phone, calls the front desk and tells them he thinks he has just seen a helicopter crash.

The pilot of helicopter No. 2, Phillip Huth, lands at 1:45 a.m. at Midway Airport in Chicago. He is worried. Helicopter No. 3 should have landed right behind him, but where is it? Furthermore, the pilots had agreed to use the same radio frequency – 123.0 – during the flight so they could talk with each other. But the last time any of them heard from Jeff Brown in helicopter No. 3 was seconds after taking off when he reported having cleared the golf course.

As Huth adds it up, he reaches a sickening conclusion – something has gone wrong. He contacts his superiors and they sound the alarm. Search and rescue operations begin immediately.

AS DAWN IS BREAKING on the misty hills around Alpine Valley Ski Resort, an Air Force search helicopter picks up the beacon from an emergency locater transmitter. The crew homes in on the signal and follows it to an open hillside – a man-made ski slope. Fifty feet below the summit among the Bittersweet and Queen Anne's lace, they find a 250-foot swath of carnage – the scattered remnants of helicopter No. 3 and the bodies of its five occupants. Clapton and Jimmy are called to identify the victims – employees, friends and family.

THE NTSB INVESTIGATED to figure out why the well-maintained helicopter flown by an experience pilot hit the ground in a *"high energy, high velocity impact at a shallow angle."* They determined the helicopter flew less than a mile and at a lower altitude than the others before crashing 100 feet above its take-off point and just 50 feet below the top of the hill. After exhaustive tests on the helicopter, they found *"no pre-impact failure or malfunction."* There was no problem with the helicopter.

They noted witness reports of haze and fog in the area but also noted the other pilots reported acceptable visibility. In the end, the NTSB blamed the pilot for *"improper planning/decision making... and his failure to attain adequate altitude before flying over rising terrain at night."*

According to the NTSB, as Brown left the take-off zone, blinded by *"darkness, fog, haze...and lack of visual cues,"* he simply did not see the terrain rising in front of him and flew the helicopter full speed into the hillside.

STEVIE WAS BURIED in a private ceremony at Laurel Land Cemetery in Dallas on Aug. 31, 1990. The mourners were a who's who of Rock and Blues royalty. More than 3,000 fans gathered outside the chapel.

On Nov. 21, 1993, the city of Austin erected a statue honoring him. It stands near the site of his last Austin concert.

Oddities and Ironies

STEVIE DIED exactly four years after his father.

The NTSB ordered toxicology tests on all of the victims of the crash. Stevie's came back clean. He had held on to the sobriety for which he had worked so hard all the way until the end.

Alcoholics Anonymous awards a "chip" each year on the anniversary of a person's sobriety. Tommy continues to pick up Stevie's chip for him.

Stevie played the Blues but, off stage, his practical jokes were legendary and apparently extended to the aliases he used when checking into hotels on tour. Some that have been reported: Ben T. Fender, Lee Melone, Mosey Long, Iza B. Klean.

In 1998 in Duluth, Minn., a man pleaded guilty to murder after stabbing his victim 42 times with a screwdriver. The murderer said he killed the man because the victim said Stevie Ray Vaughan "wasn't any good."

The album Stevie had recorded with his brother, Jimmy, *Family Style*, was released in October 1990 and entered the charts at No. 7, his biggest hit ever.

SING WITH THE WIND...

John Denver

Died: Oct. 12, 1997, Monterey Bay, Calif.

THE FAIR-HAIRED GOLDEN BOY of 1970s Country-Pop slips into the safety harness of an ultra-modern, experimental airplane for a pleasure flight up the rocky California coast.

It is the kind of gentle afternoon – calm of air and clear of clouds – that has beckoned pilots across the decades to toss the dusty canvasses from their Jennys and Pietenpols, Pipers and Cessnas, to forget their earthbound cares for solitude and serenity among the creatures of the sky. Today, John Denver hears the call.

He coaxes his airplane from the runway, and turns toward the afternoon sun, climbing ever higher to ride the wind above sea.

John, 53 years old, has already passed beyond the pinnacle of professional success and through the abyss of personal failure. However, high above the jagged shoreline today, neither is of consequence. Those equal imposters have vanished with the runway behind him.

Flying has that effect on John. Throughout his life, he has found both peace and liberation within the snug confines of a cozy cockpit. Through the bubble canopy today, the sun shines, literally, on his shoulders and he is one with the beckoning wind.

A moment later, John would be dead, his body shattered along with his airplane in the shallow waters of Monterey Bay.

John Denver

PERHAPS HENRY JOHN DEUTSCHENDORF came by his love of flying genetically. He was born the son of an U.S. Air Force pilot on New Year's Eve 1943. Although it was music that later made him rich and famous, it was flying that captivated him early in life. He abandoned the guitar his grandmother gave him because practice was tedious, but flying appealed to his sense of adventure and grandeur.

As a teenager, John attended Texas Tech with the intention of becoming an architect. But it was the early 1960s and Elvis was transforming pop culture with a wiggle and guitar, and like millions of other teenagers, John suddenly embraced the instrument that had so bored him earlier. To the dismay of his parents, he abandoned his classes, headed to Los Angeles, changed his name and became a Folk singer.

His break came when he won a national competition to replace Chad Mitchell in the Chad Mitchell Trio. John's clear tenor blended perfectly with the other two singers and his songwriting was a happy bonus. He stayed with the Mitchell Trio until after the last original member left. By the time John departed for a solo career in 1969, the group had morphed into Denver, Boise and Johnson.

That year the legendary folk trio Peter, Paul and Mary, recorded *I'm Leaving on a Jet Plane*, a plaintive tune John had written about the loneliness and isolation of touring. *I'm Leaving on a Jet Plane* became a monster hit for Peter, Paul and Mary, and the launch pad for John's solo career.

Over the next decade he would score hit after hit – 9 top singles, 14 gold albums, and 8 platinum albums. His status as an all-round entertainer was solidified by the successful television special *An Evening with John Denver* in 1975, and his starring role opposite George Burns in the 1978 movie *Oh God!*

John enjoyed "cross-over" popularity – a successful Pop singer who then established a devoted Country music following, but he did it at his own peril.

In the mid-1970s, Nashville was pushing a slick "Country-politan" sound and, ironically, some Nashville insiders were offended by outsider John's more "natural" country sound. When he won the Country Music Association's Entertainer of the Year Award and Song of the Year Award for *Back Home Again*, Charlie Rich pulled John's name from the envelope, then pulled a lighter from his pocket and burned it.

Though he continued to make hit records for several more years, by the early 1980s, John's popularity on the radio had begun to wane. He still sold out concert tickets, but fewer and fewer records.

Eventually, RCA Records dropped him.

With his sandy hair and wire-rimmed glasses, John had been the 1970s poster boy for wholesomeness. However, as his recording career dimmed, a darker side emerged – two bitter divorces, alcoholism and multiple arrests for drunken driving.

Because of his drunken driving arrests – one in 1993, another in 1994 – the Federal Aviation Administration informed John that to continue flying he would have to stop drinking altogether.

When he failed to do that, they ruled John was no longer fit to fly. Whether he ever learned of that ruling remains unclear.

The first letter sent by the FAA to inform him was returned unclaimed. A receipt for a second letter was returned, but the signature was illegible.

The question of a proper medical certificate notwithstanding, John's enormous success provided him with the means to indulge his passion for aviation. He continued to fly, and buy, airplanes. He owned a variety of them over the years, and had been certified to fly just about anything that would.

His airman certificate contained an impressive list of qualifications, including those needed for single-engine airplanes, multi-engine airplanes, gliders and Lear Jets.

He especially enjoyed the freedom of aerobatic flight and perhaps the dare-devilry of it too. As the *L.A. Times* reported: "Joe Frazier, who played with John in the Chad Mitchell Trio folk group of the 1960s, remembers scary moments in a bi-plane that seemed at times to scrape the mountain peaks and nuzzle the valley floors around Aspen." And John's former manager, Tim Mooney, recalls a favorite antic: the singer would cut the engine 35 miles from the landing strip and then glide in.

"He flew anything with wings and an engine on it," Mooney said, "from stunt planes to jets to Piper Cubs in the Alaskan bush."

His love of aerobatic flight led John to become a spokesman for the Experimental Aircraft Association's Young Eagle Program – an effort to get young people involved in aviation. EAA President Tom Poberezny felt John's enthusiasm for aviation, and aerobatics in particular, made him the perfect person to pitch aviation to the pilots of tomorrow.

However, John wanted more than the exhilaration of aerobatic flight. He wanted to take the freedom of flight about which he had written so lyrically in song to its ultimate conclusion. He longed for the wonder, solitude, and weightlessness of space.

In the early 1980s, the U.S. space program was launching shuttles into orbit with monotonous regularity. To regenerate flagging enthusiasm, NASA decided to send a civilian into orbit aboard the Space Shuttle *Challenger*.

John lobbied hard for the slot, and in 1989 told the *Nashville Tennessean*, "I was actually the catalyst for the whole 'Civilians in Space' program. I had virtually been told that the first flight was mine until President Reagan said he was going to send a teacher first."

The President's decision disappointed John, and saved his life. *The Challenger* exploded in the cold blue sky of a South Florida morning, killing all aboard, including schoolteacher Sharon Christa McAuliffe. John wrote the song *Flying for Me* as a musical memorial.

If John could not go into space, he would wring from wings and propellers all of the adventure possible. And there were some people in the Mojave Desert who were doing that better than everybody else.

In 1974, Burt Rutan abandoned his career testing jets for the Air Force and moved to the cheapest place he could find, Mojave, Calif., to chase a dream. He had designed a radical looking aircraft when he was still an engineering student at Cal PolyTech. He called it the VariViggen and after all these years, it was time to see if it would fly.

It was a strange bird that appeared to fly backwards. There was an odd little tail – called a "canard" – in front where the engine should be. The main wings were in the rear; even stranger, the engine and propeller were back there too. To many people it looked more like a practical joke than a serious flying machine.

But it not only flew, it flew well, and the snickering subsided over the succeeding decades as Rutan's radical designs brought forth some of the more significant aviation innovations since a couple of bicycle builders flew their contraption at Kitty Hawk.

Rutan popularized the use of composites instead of metal, and, of course, that strange little, front-mounted wing – the canard. His company, Rutan Aircraft Factory, was not so much a factory as a design shop, and a prolific one. RAF turned out an impressive list of airplane designs – not the airplanes themselves, just the designs.

However, anyone with the time, desire, and resources could purchase the blueprints for their favorite plane and build it in their own garage. One of the more popular homebuilt designs was for a sleek, two-seater called the Long EZ. It was nimble and fast. And John wanted one.

So, too, did Adrian Davis. He purchased plans for a Long EZ from Rutan Aircraft Factory and built the plane himself. On June 12, 1987, a Federal Aviation Administration inspector from the Houston, Texas, Flight Standards District Office examined Davis' work and approved the airplane for an airworthiness certificate in the "amateur-built, experimental category."

As the name implies, the "amateur-built, experimental category" allowed the builder the freedom to experiment and be creative with his work. Davis took advantage of that to deviate from Rutan's blueprints and re-route some fuel lines to the rear of the airplane and to mount a larger engine on it than called for in the operator's manual.

Rutan designed the Long EZ for either a 100-horse-power Continental 0-200 or a 115 horsepower Lycoming 0-235 engine. But Davis mounted on the rear of the plane a Lycoming

0-320-E3D – a 150- horsepower engine. The additional horse-power would make the hotshot little plane even hotter, but burn fuel faster.

Davis flew his Long EZ until March 5, 1994, when he sold it to Santa Ynes veterinarian Van E. Snow. During the time Snow owned the Long EZ, he lent it to his friend Klaus Savier and, in exchange for use of the plane, Savier agreed to "hop it up." Savier was so pleased with his work that he flew the plane from his home in Santa Paula, Calif., to Lakeland, Fla., and entered it in the Sun 60 Race, a closed course speed race flown at low altitude – a dangerous event that for Savier was about to become even more so.

SPEEDING LOW THROUGH THE COURSE, Savier hears the engine sput-ter and quit. Only a few hundred feet above the ground, he has mere seconds to switch from the empty fuel tank to the other and re-light the engine. Desperate to gain vital altitude, he yanks back on the stick, then, lunges for the fuel control switch handle, but the shoulder harness stops him. He snaps loose the buckle, turns 90 degrees in the seat, reaches behind his left shoulder, and grabs the handle – but is confounded by what he sees.

It's not clear which end of the handle is the "pointer" and, furthermore, the markings for the fuel tank positions are illogi-cal – the handle in the "right" position feeds fuel from the left tank, the "down" position feeds from the right tank, and "up" is for off! As the airplane falls, Savier frantically rotates the handle until fuel begins flowing from the full fuel tank, and with only seconds to spare, the engine sputters to life. He shoves the throt-tle forward and, as the airspeed indicator needle finally begins to rise, he initiates a climb and narrowly avoids catastrophe.

After the race, Savier tells Snow the fuel selector handle – its placement (behind and to the left of the pilot's seat), and its confusing markings – are "bad news" and should be fixed.

BY FALL 1997, SNOW HAD DECIDED TO SELL his Long EZ, and John was eager to buy one. The deal was consummated Sept. 27, 1997, and the plane was flown to Santa Maria, Calif., where it spent the next two weeks being sanded, primed, and painted in a new multi-color paint scheme.

ON OCT. 11, 1997, JOHN PICKS UP the Long EZ and flies it to its new home at the Monterey airport where he stores it in a hangar.

The next day John, relaxed in cowboy boots, sweater and base-ball cap, arrives at the airport eager to become better acquainted with his new toy.

Its sleek lines, canard wing, and rear-mounted "pusher-prop," make it look more like a ride for Luke Skywalker than a Folk-singer. Mechanic Chris Hadland helps John tug it from the hangar into the October sun where they admire the little plane.

It's the aviation equivalent of a hotshot sports car – not a brute-strength American muscle car, more a slick European design in which form is as meaningful as function. John is eager to take it for a spin up the coast, perhaps buzz his friend Clint Eastwood's house.

He examines the wings for dings, dents, dirt or deformities – anything that could disrupt the airflow and keep lift at bay, and he pays special attention to the canard – that small, strange wing at the front of the airplane.

Although it gives the plane an exotic, futuristic look, the "tail first" design actually goes all the way back to Wilbur and Orville's "Wright Flyer."

John borrows a cup from Hadland, crouches beneath the

plane and drains an ounce or two of fuel from the sump. He holds the clear container against the light, examines the pale blue fuel for contaminates – rust, dirt, bugs, anything that might block a fuel line and stop the airplanes lifeblood, 100 octane Avgas, from flowing freely to the engine. Finding no contaminants, John pours the sample on the tarmac and continues inspecting the airplane.

He lifts the bubble canopy and points out to Hadland the odd placement of a handle in the cockpit.

The handle is attached to the "fuel selector valve" – a mechanism that determines which of the Long EZ fuel tanks — there is one in each wing — is feeding the engine. The pilot selects the tank from which to draw fuel by turning the handle on the value. The blueprint calls for this valve to be located handily between the pilot's knees, offering quick and easy access should it become necessary to switch tanks in flight.

However, there is nothing that requires the builder of a "homebuilt" experimental airplane to follow the blueprints and the builder of this particular Long EZ did not. Instead of placing the fuel selector valve in the cockpit, he isolated it with the engine behind the rear bulkhead in the back of the plane. But, of course, a pilot sitting in the front cockpit would not be able to reach the valve's handle way back there. So, he concocted a system of rods and universal joints that ran from the fuel control valve in the back of the plane forward through the rear bulkhead and to a handle that he placed on the front bulkhead.

The front bulkhead also serves as the pilot's seat back. This "remote" handle is positioned behind and to the left of the pilot's left shoulder. By turning this remote fuel selector handle, the pilot actuates the fuel valve in the rear of the airplane. The innovation is as noble in intent as it is convoluted in design.

Fire aboard an airplane is unlike a fire in a car. Should your car catch fire, you simply pull over and call your insurance agent. In a plane cruising at 10,000 feet, the option of "just pulling over" simply does not exist.

As the crew and passengers discovered in the crash of ValuJet Flight 592 in the Florida Everglades, while you are "pulling over" – descending to the nearest airport – the cabin is filling with smoke and fire, scorching your lungs, obscuring your vision, and burning you alive.

FEW EVENTS EVOKE STARK TERROR in the hearts of pilots like a fire in the cockpit. That's why pilots tend to pay special attention to the fuel control valve. In addition to determining which tank is feeding the engine, it can be turned to shut off the fuel flow altogether. In case of a fire in the engine compartment, the pilot simply turns the handle to "off," stops the flow of fuel and starves the fire.

But there is a problem with fuel control valves.

They resemble a small octopus with fuel lines for tentacles – two flexible hoses reaching from the valve to the fuel tanks in each wing with another hose running from the valve to the engine. A breech of one of these lines could spew high-octane aviation fuel through the cockpit, and the terrified pilot would have little choice but to wait helplessly for the slightest ignition – a static spark, a hot wire – to turn the plane into which he is strapped into a fireball plummeting like a meteor from the sky.

Fearful of such an event, the builder of John's Long EZ deviated from the original Rutan design. Using his Rube Goldbergish system of rods, joints and a remote handle, he cleverly routed the fuel valve and its tangle of fuel lines away from the cockpit and isolated them in the rear of the plane. No fuel lines in the cockpit – no cockpit catastrophe.

JOHN REACHES IN TO TURN the fuel selector's remote handle and discovers that not only is it awkward to reach, it is also difficult to budge. Hadland retrieves a pair of vice grip pliers from the shop and attaches them to the balky handle, hoping to encourage it by increasing leverage. However, John realizes, even with the vice grips attached, the handle still will be beyond reach once he is buckled tightly into the safety harness.

He dismisses the problem, saying should the need arise to switch tanks in-flight, he will simply engage the auto pilot to fly the airplane while he unbuckles and turns around to wrestle with the reluctant handle. He will have it moved to a more convenient place in the cockpit while he is on tour next week, he says, but for today, he will live with it as it is.

John climbs into the forward of the two front-to-back cockpits and continues his pre-flight inspection of the aircraft – checking controls and gauges. Hadland, standing nearby, notices another oddity about this airplane. The fuel gauges are placed on the sidewalls of the rear cockpit and cannot be seen by the pilot in front. So, John asks Hadland to look in the rear cockpit and read the fuel gauges for him.

The fuel gauges are clear vertical tubes. Fuel lifts a small red ball inside to indicate the amount of fuel in the tank, much like mercury rises and falls in a thermometer to indicate temperature. But, unlike a thermometer, which has gradient markings along the side to denote the temperature in degrees that a particular level of mercury represents, the fuel gauges on this plane do not have marking to denote the gallons of fuel in the tank that a particular level of fuel in the tube represents. Without those markings, it is natural to assume that the level of fuel in the tube corresponds equally to the amount of fuel in the tank – half a tube of fuel would mean half a tank of fuel.

It is a logical assumption – but it's wrong.

The red ball in the left fuel gauge, Hadland says, shows less than a quarter full and the red ball in the right fuel gauge shows less than a half. Hadland offers to bring over the fuel pump truck and add some fuel, but John declines. He is eager to go fly this little sports car-of-an-airplane.

According to the gauges, there is more than enough fuel for the hour-long flight John envisions.

But, the fuel gauges are not indicating a half-full tank in the right wing tank and a quarter full tank in the left wing tank. On these particular gauges, the level of fuel showing in the tube does not correspond equally with the amount of fuel in the tanks, but, tragically, there are no markings to make that clear.

So, while both John and Hadland believe the fuel gauges are showing the airplane has about 19 gallons of fuel on board (1/2 full right tank – 13 gallons; 1/4 full left tank – 6.5 gallons), in fact, there are fewer – far fewer.

HAD JOHN CONSIDERED the Long EZ's recent flight history, he might have better understood how little fuel was in the tanks. The day before he had flown in his Lear Jet to the paint shop at the airport in Santa Maria to inspect the airplane and fly it back to Monterey. He was thrilled with the plane's new look and thanked everyone in the shop by taking them out for lunch. Later in the day, John and pilot Eric Cobb returned to the Santa Maria airport where Cobb gave John a half-hour checkout flight in the Long EZ.

Cobb was so impressed with John's flying skills that he had John make a second landing just to prove the first one, which was perfect, wasn't a fluke.

Confident in John's flying abilities, but concerned about the amount of fuel in the plane, Cobb warned John that he had exactly 10 gallons of fuel in the right wing tank, and 5 gallons, or 30 minutes of fuel in the left wing tank, and that he should think of the 5-gallon side as strictly reserve fuel.

Late that afternoon John flew the airplane back to Monterey – another serene communion with the wind. The hour-long flight burned about 10 gallons of fuel, leaving on-board only 5 gallons.

So, now, having misunderstood the fuel gauges, John believes there is enough fuel for nearly two hours flight, but there is actually only enough for about thirty minutes.

HADLAND HANDS JOHN a small mirror to keep an eye on the gauges behind him and returns to the hangar to put away his tools. He hears the engine fire up with a throaty roar, run for a few seconds, then quit.

Stepping to the door, he sees John turned left in his seat toward the balky fuel handle. A moment later John restarts the engine and gives the mechanic a "no problem" wave.

John closes the bubble canopy and muffles the outside roar. Snug in the fighter-jet-like cockpit, he tunes the aircraft radio to the ground control frequency and keys the microphone, identifying himself by the Long EZ's "N" number — N555JD — which John had specially requested from the FAA to incorporate his own initials.

John: Ground (control) this is, uh, five five five Juliet Delta at the big hangar at, uh, Delmonte East. (Request permission to)Taxi for take-off with information.

Ground Controller: Long Easy five five five Juliet Delta, Monterey Ground, taxi to runway two eight left and say direction or destination as requested.

John: Uh, runway two eight left and I'm going to stay in the pattern, uh, and do some, uh, touch and goes.

Ground Controller: Long Easy five Juliet Delta squawk one two zero zero and taxi to runway two eight left ... and, uh, Tower will assign pattern direction and landing runway.

John: Thank you very much, sir.

John taxis the Long EZ to the end of runway 28 Left – the west departure runway. He completes his final "pre-departure" checklist then dials in a different radio frequency to call the airport's Control Tower and keys the mic again.

John: Tower, this is Long Easy triple five Juliet Delta, ready for takeoff, two eight left. Like to stay in the pattern and do some landings, touch and goes.

Tower: Long Easy triple five Juliet Delta, Monterey Tower, hold short of the runway, landing traffic.

John: Roger, Juliet Delta.

John waits on the taxiway and watches another airplane touch down, roll to the far end, and exit. The Tower calls John and tells him to move his airplane onto the runway and await instructions.

Tower: Long Easy five Juliet Delta, runway two eight left, taxi into position and hold.

John: Position and hold.

John eases the throttle forward. The small plane creeps to the centerline of the runway and pivots west toward Monterey Bay. He stops and waits. In front of him, beyond the canopy, nose cone, and canard, lays a mile and a half stretch of runway and, beyond that, a place in the distance where the blue Pacific blends seamlessly with the autumn sky, all of it bathed in the amber glow of late afternoon.

It's a beautiful day to go flying.

Unseen in the gauge behind him, the red ball vibrates atop an alarmingly short column of fuel.

Tower: Long Easy Five Juliet Delta, make right closed traffic, runway two eight left. Cleared for take off.

John pushes the throttle forward and, as fuel gushes into the over-sized engine, the nimble plane responds aggressively. He releases the brakes and the rear-facing prop spins up and pushes the plane down the runway … 40 miles an hour, 50, 70, 80 … John keys the microphone.

John: Juliet Delta on the roll. Thank you.

He squeezes back the control handle at the end of the right armrest and the canard lifts the front wheel off the pavement. It rotates up and tilts John against the seatback – his head resting inches from the remote fuel control handle. A moment later, the main landing gear beneath the wings unsticks and John points the plane slightly above the horizon, climbing at 120 miles an hour.

Instead of flying straight away, he stays in "the pattern" – an imaginary rectangle which overlays the airport. At about 1,000 feet, he banks right to fly the first short leg of the rectangle, then another right turn puts him on the long downwind leg, parallel to the runway.

As he passes the end of the runway, John pulls back on the throttle lever, restricting fuel flow and reducing power slightly. He turns right again for the base leg and descends toward a final slow right turn, aligning the small plane with the runway. He pulls back the throttle even more and brings the small plane down the final approach slope to the runway, aiming for the number "28" painted on the pavement.

As the wheels touch down, John presses the throttle full forward, sucking a surge of gas from the quickly draining fuel tank and into the engine's four cylinders. Reaching take-off speed, he pulls back on the control stick and the Long EZ hops off the runway – airborne again.

John repeats the "Touch and Go" two more times. It's a safe way to learn the unfamiliar airplane, since the process of taking off, flying the pattern, and landing requires him to test its most fundamental capabilities – climbs, turns and descents – and it's all done close enough to the airport for an easy glide to a safe runway if, God forbid, the engine should quit.

After the third touch down John hits the throttle, accelerates, and pulls the Long EZ back into the air. Now confident in the new airplane, and in his abilities with it, it is time to leave the safe confines of the pattern and go flying.

As he climbs away from the runway, John is unaware that in the cockpit behind him, the red ball has dropped to the bottom of the tube.

John: Tower, Juliet Delta would like to continue straight out, take a flight around the point if I may.

The Tower tells John to tune his transponder – an on-board radio that transmits information about his flight (such as speed and altitude) onto their radar screens – to a particular code number or squawk.

Tower: Long Easy Five Juliet Delta, roger, squawk zero three six seven.

John: Zero three six seven, thank you.

However, the air traffic controller sees nothing on his radar screen except the Primary Radar signal – the simple echo return from the sweep of the radar dish, which shows John's airplane as a "blip" leaving the airport and headed toward the bay. So, he calls John on the radio.

Tower: Long Easy five Juliet Delta, I'm not receiving your transponder.

John: How about now, sir?

Tower: Thank you, I have it.

John keys his mic again, but the transmission is unintelligible.

Those enjoying a day at the shore hear a high pitch whine in the distance and notice a strange-looking airplane skimming up the coast just a few hundred feet off shore. Suddenly, the whining engine sputters.

The air traffic controller calls John again, but gets no response.

John's attention is riveted to the sudden silence. The roar of the engine has been replaced by the stark whisper of the air stream passing over the canopy.

Can't be out of gas, can it? With mere seconds to restart the engine before the plane hits the water, he grabs for the oddly placed remote fuel selector handle to switch tanks, but the shoulder harness won't let him reach it. Quickly, he releases the control stick, unbuckles frantically and flings off the shoulder harness. He pivots left in his seat and lunges for the awkwardly placed fuel control handle. He struggles with the handle, but it resists. Desperately pressing, pulling, pivoting around even further in his seat, he inadvertently depresses the right rudder pedal.

Focused on the handle, he fails to see the water rushing towards him.

On shore, they watch as the silent airplane noses up, rolls over then plunges into Monterey Bay. That part of the airplane that survives impact with the water is destroyed on an outcropping of rocks beneath the surface.

JOHN'S REMAINS ARE RECOVERED QUICKLY but not identified until the next day. They are cremated and taken to his beloved Aspen, Colorado.

On the following Friday, Oct. 17, 1997, more than 2,000 people gathered at Faith Presbyterian Church in Aurora, Colo., to say goodbye to John. His sometimes sentimental, sometimes sunny songs had touched the hearts of millions. John's own prescient song, *On the Wings of a Dream*, played at the service, asked the very questions with which those hearts now ached, "Why is it thus we are here and so soon we are gone?"

IN ITS FINAL REPORT, the NTSB determined the probable cause of the crash was *"The pilot's diversion of attention from the operation of the airplane and his inadvertent application of right rudder that resulted in the loss of airplane control while attempting to manipulate the fuel selector handle. In addition, the Board determined that the pilot's inadequate preflight planning and preparation, specifically his failure to refuel the airplane, was causal. The Board determined that the builder's decision to locate the unmarked fuel selector handle in a hard-to-access position, unmarked fuel quantity sight gauges, inadequate transition training by the pilot, and his lack of total experience in this type of airplane were factors in the accident."*

According to the NTSB, John failed to follow the cardinal rule of piloting: First, fly the airplane. In flight training, that rule is repeated like a mantra. If the plane is on fire, if the propeller falls off, if an alien spaceship is sucking you into a time warp, first, fly the airplane. When John let go of the control stick, and turned to grapple with the fuel control handle, he stopped flying the airplane and was smitten by fate for breaking the cardinal rule.

Had he only continued to fly the airplane once the engine went silent, he might have ditched safely in the ocean, popped open the canopy and continued to enjoy the sunshine on his shoulders while being towed in by the shore patrol.

WHILE THE NTSB INVESTIGATION of John's crash answers many questions, it also raises some troubling ones. Why would John fly an experimental – one of a kind – airplane in which he had so little training? According the NTSB, aside from a couple of demonstration rides, John had only 30 minutes of training in N555JD. Maybe that is enough as long as everything goes well, but it is difficult to believe with such truncate training a pilot could become so intimately familiar with the airplane's systems he could react by rote when the chips are down.

Why would John choose to fly an airplane with a fuel selector about which he was so concerned and had already resolved to have it fixed?

Why would John fly an airplane, particularly one in which he had so little experience, with only partially filled fuel tanks?

Why, when mechanic Hadland offered to bring over the fuel truck and add more fuel, did John decline?

And finally, why did he fly at so low an altitude that he had only seconds to solve a problem?

Only John knows the answers, and perhaps he would be here to tell us, if only first, he had flown the airplane.

Oddities and Ironies

THE LONG EZ is not built of metal. It is actually built of foam wrapped in fiberglass. Had John ditched his airplane in the water, he might well have sailed to shore.

Aside from being an internationally known singer, John was

also an internationally known environmentalist and conservationist. He established the Windstar Foundation to promote environmental and conservation projects and awareness. Ironically, the area of Monterey Bay in which John crashed is a wildlife sanctuary.

During the 1970s gas crisis, John was widely rumored to have installed a couple of large gas tanks at his home to ensure he would have plenty of gas. Twenty years later, he would die because his plane ran out.

The FAA's concern with John's alcohol problem, ultimately, was unwarranted. Toxicology tests after the crash showed John had no alcohol in his system at the time of the accident.

Investigators initially thought John's plane might have crashed as a result of hitting a bird in flight. Feathers were found embedded in the wreckage. That theory vanished when Cobb, the pilot who had "checked out" John in the Long EZ, explained that John had trouble reaching the rudder pedals. To help move John a bit forward and closer to the pedals, Cobb had given him a pillow to put behind his back – a down pillow.

John was taught to fly by one of the best – his father. On Jan. 12, 1962, Maj. Henry J. Deutschendorf, Sr., set two air-speed records and was named to the Air Force Hall of Fame at Edwards AFB, Calif.

John played what was to be his last concert in Corpus Christi, Texas, on Oct. 5, 1997. His encore that night (and the final song of his performing life) was his hit *Calypso* – an ode to the sea. A week later, he would die there.

ONE IN A MILLION...

Aaliyah

Died: Aug. 25, 2001, Marsh Harbour Airport, Abaco Island

THE PILOT IS HAVING NONE OF IT. With nine people on board and gas in the tanks, the airplane is already going to be dangerously close to its maximum weight limit. The passengers can complain all they like, but they will have to leave their bags behind. Even a twin engine airplane like the Cessna 402 has its limits. It's just too dangerous to fly if the airplane's over-weight, and this one is.

The passengers will just have to understand.

However, these are no ordinary passengers. Aaliyah is one of the faster rising stars in R&B, and her entourage includes body guard Scott Gallin, manager Keith Wallace, record executive Gina Smith, make-up artist Eric Foreman, video director Douglas Kratz and hairstylists Anthony Dodd and Christopher Maldonado. They have spent the past several days in the Bahamas filming Aaliyah's new music video and are eager to get on board and begin their trip home.

Eventually, they prevail upon the pilot and cram themselves and their luggage into the twin-engine airplane for the flight to

Opa-Locka, Fla.

Pilot Luis Morales taxis to runway 27, pushes the throttles forward and at 6:50 p.m. the airplane lumbers down asphalt. Slowly it rises but struggles to climb. Suddenly, just as it passes beyond the runway, it dives nose first, slams into the marsh and explodes. The impact and explosion ejects several of the passengers, still strapped to their seats.

Six of the nine on board die instantly, including Aaliyah. Three others survive the impact and fire only to die a short time later.

BORN JAN. 16, 1979, she was named Aaliyah, Arabic for "most exalted," and by the age of 22, Aaliyah Dana Haughton would become exactly that in the world of R&B.

She was born in New York, but grew up in Detroit. Hers was a musical household. Her mother was a talented singer and kept the house filled with popular music. As though by osmosis, Aaliyah absorbed the songs of Stevie Wonder, Marvin Gaye and others, and then sang the songs for family and friends.

At age 11, she secured a spot on *Star Search,* but her version of *Funny Valentine* failed to impress the judges. However, a bigger opportunity lay just ahead.

Aaliyah's aunt-by-marriage, legendary singer Gladys Knight, invited the 11-year-old to perform with her at Bally's Casino in Las Vegas. With Gladys as her mentor, Aaliyah's four-night stint at Bally's became a master's class in live performing.

Gladys' husband, Aaliyah's uncle Barry Hankerson, followed Aaliyah's career carefully for the next couple of years and signed her to his Blackground Records label when she was 13. He assigned artist R. Kelly to produce and write most of the songs for her first album, *Age Ain't Nothing but a Number.*

Two songs from the album, *Back and Forth* and *At Your Best*

(You Are Love), shot to the top of the charts and made Aaliyah a star at 15. The album produced two more hits: *Down with the Clique* and the title track *Age Ain't Nothing but a Number*, and eventually went platinum.

Perhaps reading too much into the album's title, some questioned 15-year-old Aaliyah's relationship with 25-year-old R. Kelly. There were even reports the two had married. Both vigorously denied the marriage rumors and insisted they were merely personal friends and professional collaborators.

Their relationship, whatever it was, was over by the time Aaliyah recorded her sophomore album in 1996. For *One in a Million*, Aaliyah worked with producers Missy Elliot and Timbaland. With the hits *If Your Girl Only Knew, One in a Million, Hot like Fire, The One I Gave My Heart To, 4 Page Letter* and the remake of a Marvin Gaye song, *Got to Give it Up*, the album was a smash success.

After the release of *One in a Million*, Aaliyah turned her attention to a new area of the music business – movie soundtracks. She was nominated for an Oscar for the song, *Journey Through the Past* from the movie *Anastasia* and then nominated for a Grammy for the song, *Are You That Somebody*, from the *Dr. Doolittle* soundtrack.

Her interest in the movie business expanded from singing soundtracks to acting. Critics gave her favorable notices for her movie-acting debut in *Romeo Must Die*. She parlayed that success into deals to act in the *Matrix II* and *Matrix III*, the Anne Rice movie *Queen of the Damned* and the made-for-television movie *Some Kind of Blue*.

After taking time off to "rejuvenate" and get her "creative juices flowing again," Aaliyah released her third album, *AALIYAH*. Like the others before it, the *AALIYAH* album shot to the top of the charts. In late August 2001, Aaliyah flew to the Bahamas to shoot a video for the single *Rock the Boat,* which was to be released from the album.

It was an all-day shoot beginning at 3 a.m. A documentary crew from BET network captured much of it for a behind-the-scenes special. Aaliyah and her video crew had planned to work the next day, but the shoot went so well they wrapped by late afternoon.

Eager to return home, Aaliyah and the others decided to fly back early, rather than the next day as planned. But the last minute change of plans required them to change charter flights, too. Rather than flying home with the charter service that had ferried them to the island, they hired a different charter with a smaller airplane.

The airplane was a twin engine Cessna 402. Cessna produced the 402 for 17 years between 1968 and 1985. With room for eight, it is a common choice for air-taxi flight services. Its two turbo-charged 325-horsepower engines can push the airplane above 25,000 feet at speeds of more than 200 miles an hour.

But no airplane can carry unlimited weight, and by the time Aaliyah and her passengers boarded the Cessna 402 it was several hundred pounds over its limit.

According to the Bahamian government's Civil Aviation Department, the Cessna 402 was certified to take off with a maximum weight of 6,300 pounds. It weighed 4,117 pounds empty. The luggage recovered from the site (except one bag which sank in the marsh) weighed 574 pounds. It was carrying 804 pounds of fuel. That left only 805 pounds to spare before adding passengers, one of whom weighed nearly 300 pounds.

According to the NTSB *"The total weight of the luggage, fuel on board at the time of the accident, plus the weight of the passengers showed that the total gross weight of the airplane was sub-*

stantially exceeded."

Perhaps more significant was the NTSB finding that the weight was not properly distributed throughout the airplane. *"Preliminary center of gravity calculations showed that the center of gravity was significantly outside the flight envelope past the aft center of gravity."*

Simply stated, the airplane was "tail heavy," making it extremely difficult for the pilot to control.

And the pilot at the controls was not authorized to be there. According to The Associated Press, the Federal Aviation Administration had authorized a different pilot, not Morales, to act as pilot for the air-taxi service.

The specifics of what caused the airplane to nose-dive into the marsh shortly after take-off might be debated for some time to come. However, what happened next is indisputable: Aaliyah's latest album, *AALIYAH*, which had debuted on the charts at No. 2 in early July, had fallen to No. 27 by late August. The week of the crash, it jumped up eight positions to No. 19 and eventually sold more than two and a half million copies.

Next, upon its release less than a year later, Aaliyah's movie *Queen of the Damned* became the No. 1 movie in America. Aaliyah's rising star continued to rise long after the star, herself, had fallen from the Bahamian sky.

ON AUG. 31, 2001, a horse-drawn, glass-paneled carriage carried Aaliyah's silver coffin through the streets of Manhattan's Upper West Side to the St. Ignatius Loyola Roman Catholic Church where thousands had gathered to pay their final respects. Twenty-two white doves were released, one to mark each year of an exalted life.

"...YOU KNOW THEY'VE GOTTA HAVE A HELL OF A BAND..."

Joe Dan Petty
Grinderswitch Bassist,
Allman Brothers Guitar Tech

Died: Jan. 8, 2000, Macon, Ga.

JOE DAN PETTY FIRST CAME TO ROCK 'N ROLL as a "roadie" for the Allman Brothers. It was his job to set up Butch Trucks' drums before live performances. Then, with the rise of the Southern Rock phenomenon in the early 1970s, Joe Dan joined Dru Lombar, Larry Howard, Rick Burnett and Stephen Miller to create the blues/rock band Grinderswitch. Grinderswitch released their first album, *Honest to Goodness,* in 1974 and spent most of the mid-1970s recording and touring.

They frequently opened for major Southern Bands including The Allman Brothers, The Marshall Tucker Band, Wet Willie and Lynyrd Skynyrd. Their albums of that period – *Honest to Goodness* (1974); *Macon Tracks* (1975); *Pullin' Together* (1977); and *Redwing* (1977) – were well-received. However, Grinderswitch was never able to rise above opening act status. With the coming of Disco, Grinderswitch faded away with so many other Southern Rock bands.

Joe Dan formed another band, the Lifters. It was mostly a cover band but it kept a paycheck coming in. Then, in the early 1980s, Joe Dan returned to his old job with the Allman Brothers, this time as guitar technician.

By the late 1990s, Joe Dan had become interested in aviation. He bought a single engine Beech BE-23 and took lessons to become a private pilot.

On Jan. 8, 2000, Joe Dan and a friend, a fellow pilot, take off from Macon, Ga., from Herbert Smart Airport for a sightseeing flight. As the airplane climbs out, the engine sputters and the plane goes down through the trees about one mile from the airport.

Two young witnesses report the airplane burst into flames about five seconds after hitting the ground.

The NTSB determined the cause of the crash was "*The loss of engine power for undetermined reasons.*"

The NTSB then noted, "*A factor was conditions favorable for the formation of carburetor ice.*" (Which could have chocked off the air/fuel mixture to the engine.)

Steve Canady
Ozark Mountain Daredevils

Died: Sept. 25, 1999, Nashville, Tenn.

STEVE CANADY HAD SPENT YEARS as a member of the Ozark Mountain Daredevils, a Missouri-based band that shot to fame in the 1970s with songs like, *Jackie Blue*, and *If You Wanna Get to Heaven*. He had also worked as tour manager for Country singer and guitarist Lee Roy Parnell and Folk Rocker Marshall Chapman. By 1999, Steve was out of the music business and working for a camera shop in Nashville.

Steve had an interest in aviation that went back to his days as a helicopter pilot in Vietnam. He held a commercial pilot's license and was certified to fly both single engine and multiple engine aircraft. He had logged more than 2,000 hours of flight time.

ON SEPT. 25, 1999, Steve and Rick Loudermilk, the owner of a computer software company, go for a flight in a vintage World War II North American T-6.

Loudermilk was also a veteran pilot. He had logged more than 1,300 hours of flight time, 50 in the T-6, a trainer in which the pilot sits in the front cockpit and the co-pilot in the rear. It can be flown from either seat.

Steve climbs in the backseat and Loudermilk in the front.

They depart Nashville International Airport and head for town. As they fly over a Nashville neighborhood, they descend to between 1,000 and 800 feet when, suddenly, the airplane dives sharply, rolls inverted and cuts a swath through the treetops before hitting the ground and skidding to a stop against an apartment building.

Startled neighbors run to the wreckage and find Loudermilk dead and Steve alive but badly hurt. One neighbor uses a garden hose to extinguish a fire in the wreckage while another starts CPR on Steve.

Despite their efforts, he dies before medics can get him to the hospital.

The NTSB determined the probable cause of the accident was *"the pilot's failure to maintain flying speed which resulted in a stall and loss of control. A factor was the pilot impairment due to the use of drugs."*

Walter Hyatt
Singer/Songwriter

Died: May 5, 1996, Florida Everglades

WALTER HYATT LEFT HIS HOME IN SPARTANBURG, S.C., to become a key figure in the early days of the Austin, Texas, music scene. He became best known as the leader of Uncle Walt's Band, a Folk acoustic trio that included fellow South Carolinians Champ Hood and David Ball.

In the 1970s, their tight harmonies drew comparisons with Crosby, Stills and Nash and made them favorites on the club scene. They released two albums. Later, Walter and Hood started another band, The Contenders, but within a year had regrouped Uncle Walt's Band. The band permanently split up in 1983, although during the next few years they reunited on occasion for one-night-only performances.

Walter eventually moved to Nashville where, with the help of his old Austin pal Lyle Lovett, he plied his trade as a Country music songwriter. He continued to perform and occasionally returned to Austin to record.

In 1996, he was busy completing work on a new record.

On May 5, 1996, Walter Hyatt, and 109 others, including the flight crew, board ValuJet Flight 592 from Miami to Atlanta. The flight departs Miami at 2:03 p.m. The take-off and climb out are routine, but seven minutes into the flight there is an odd sound and a member of the flight crew asks, "What's that?"

Fourteen seconds later the captain reports, "We've got some electrical problem." There is a pause then, ominously, "We're losing everything." Seven seconds later the captain radios the air traffic controller in Miami, "We need, we need to go back to Miami."

The transmission is followed three seconds later by shouts in the background, "Fire, fire, fire. We're on fire."

The controller instructs the pilot to the turn the plane back to Miami, "Critter, five 92 (Critter is the ValuJet "call sign") ah, roger turn left heading two seven zero descend and maintain seven thousand."

A few seconds later, the controller asks the pilot the nature of the problem. The pilot responds, "Fire." The First Officer responds, "Uh, smoke in the cockp…smoke in the cabin." A few seconds later, a flight attendant shouts, "completely on fire."

At 2:11 p.m. the first officer radios the controller, requesting permission to land at the first available airport.

The controller responds, "Critter five 92 they're gonna be standing (unintelligible) standing by for you, you can plan runway one two when able direct to Dolphin (an electronic navigational aid) now." The first officer requests radar vectors (directions) and the controller provides them.

The first officer acknowledges the directions. The controller radios another set of directions, but there is no response. Then another set. The response is unintelligible. Finally, the controller radios, "Opa Locka airport's about 12 o'clock at 15 miles."

It might as well have been a million. Burning furiously from within and filled with acrid smoke, Flight 592 rolls over, points almost straight down and slams into the Everglades. It disappears in the swamp. "Uncle Walt" Hyatt and 109 others are dead.

The investigation into the ValuJet Flight 592 crash was one of the more exhaustive in NTSB history.

It concluded with the NTSB determination that the probable causes of the accident *"...which resulted from a fire in the airplane's class D cargo compartment that was initiated by the actuation of one or more oxygen generators being improperly carried as cargo, were (1) the failure of SabreTech (editor's note: the company hired to handle cargo for ValuJet) to properly prepare, package, and identify unexpended chemical oxygen generators before presenting them to ValuJet for carriage; (2) the failure of ValuJet to properly oversee its contract maintenance program to ensure compliance with maintenance, maintenance training, and hazardous materials requirements and practices; and (3) the failure of the Federal Aviation Administration (FAA) to require smoke detection and fire suppression systems in class D cargo compartments.*

"Contributing to the accident was the failure of the FAA to adequately monitor ValuJet's heavy maintenance programs and responsibilities, including ValuJet's oversight of its contractors, and SabreTech's repair station certificate; the failure of the FAA to adequately respond to prior chemical oxygen generator fires with programs to address the potential hazards; and ValuJet's failure to ensure that both ValuJet and contract maintenance facility employees were aware of the carrier's 'no-carry' hazardous materials policy and had received appropriate hazardous materials training."

Bill Graham
Rock Promoter

Died: Oct. 25, 1991, near Mill Valley, Calif.

THERE LIKELY WAS NEVER A NON-MUSICIAN more influential in the music world than Bill Graham. He was born Wolfgang Grajonca, to Russian Jews who had immigrated to Germany before his birth in 1931. When he was two days old, his father was killed in an accident. His mother put Wolfgang and five of his sisters in an orphanage. Wolfgang and one of his sisters were studying in France when Germany invaded. They fled, along with more than 60 other children and a Red Cross worker. By the time they made their way to New York, only 11, including Wolfgang, had survived. His sister had not.

In New York he was raised in a foster home, and in 1949, he changed his name to Bill Graham and became an American citizen. He studied at City College of New York and did a tour of duty during the Korean War for which he earned a Bronze Star and a Purple Heart.

Eventually, he joined two other sisters in San Francisco and tried his hand in the business world. After eight years, he abandoned the corporate life to take a job as manager of the San Francisco Mime Troupe – his entry into show business.

He created Bill Graham Presents and became the best known impresario in the business. He turned the Fillmore, a rundown auditorium in San Francisco, into THE place to attend a concert in the mid/late 1960s. He opened a Fillmore East in New York and took over Winterland, another San Francisco hall.

Along the way, he not only managed some of the top bands and promoted the top touring artists of the day, he also promoted and managed many of the more significant musical events of the last third of the 20th century, including the Live Aid benefit in 1985.

ON THE NIGHT OF OCT. 25, 1991, Bill along with his girlfriend, Melissa Gold and pilot Steve Kahn, are shuttling in a private helicopter 27 miles from a Huey Lewis and the News concert to an airport near Bill's home in Mill Valley, Calif.

According to the NTSB, Kahn, a certified airline pilot, received a weather briefing in which VFR flight was not recommended due to low ceilings and low visibility. However, since he is familiar with the geographic area, he receives a special VFR clearance and departs to the northwest.

About 20 miles from the departure point, witnesses observe the helicopter flying parallel to a highway at about 200 feet above the ground. The weather is reported to be a 200-foot overcast ceiling, gusty winds, heavy rain, and visibility of about 0.5 mile. The witnesses observe the helicopter strike the top of a 223-foot-high transmission tower and explode. The National Transportation Safety Board determined the probable cause of this accident as follows: *"The pilot's intentional flight into known adverse weather, continued flight into instrument meteorological conditions, and improper altitude. Contributing to the accident was low ceilings, poor visibility, and restricted visual lookout."*

The Reba McEntire Band

Died: March 15, 1991, San Diego

REBA MCENTIRE WAS BORN REBA NELL MCENTIRE, in Chockie, Okla., on March 28, 1955. One of four children, she begin singing with her brother and sister as the Singing McEntires.

When she sang the national anthem at a rodeo in Oklahoma City in 1974, it led to a recording contract with Mercury Records. By 1976, she had her first song on the charts: *I Don't Want to be a One Night Stand*. That same year she married her rodeo rider boyfriend, Charlie Battle.

She followed *I Don't Want to be a One Night Stand* with several other minor hits before breaking the Top 10 with *Up to Heaven*, followed by the Top 5 hit *Today All Over Again* and, in 1982, the No. 1 song *Can't Even Get the Blues*. Another No. 1 hit came her way in 1983 with the release of *You're the First Time I've Thought about Leaving*.

Her string of hits continued through the middle 1980s, reaching a pinnacle with her best-selling album and single by the same name, *Whoever's in New England*. In 1987 she divorced

Battle. Two years later, she married her bandleader, Narvel Blackstock. In 1988, she riled some Nashville traditionalists with her album, *Reba*. Some felt with songs like Otis Redding's, *Respect* and the Pop song, *A Sunday Kind of Love*, Reba was tugging Country in the wrong direction.

By 1990, Reba had expanded her career to include acting in motion pictures. Elephant gun in hand, she killed her share of Graboids in the horror movie *Tremors*. But she had not abandoned singing for the movies, and March 15, 1991, she played a private concert for IBM executives in San Diego.

ON THE AFTERNOON of March 15, 1991, the McEntire entourage arrives at San Diego's Lindbergh Field. They plan to fly after the concert that night to their next concert stop in Fort Wayne, Ind.

However, a noise curfew will be in effect at that late hour at Lindbergh field, so after the passengers disembark, the plane is flown to Brown Field, a former Naval Air Station southeast of San Diego.

After the IBM concert, seven members of Reba's band board the twin-engine Siddeley Hawker at Brown Field. Other members of the entourage board a second airplane. Reba and her husband plan to spend the night in San Diego.

The first airplane takes off at 1:40 a.m. Two minutes after taking off, it slams into the top of Otay Mountain, killing bandleader Kirk Cappello, and band members Paula Kaye Evans, Terry Jackson, Michael Thomas, Anthony Saputo, Joey Cigainero and Chris Austin, along with road manager Jim Hammon, pilot Donald Holms and co-pilot Chris Hollinger.

The NTSB determined the probable cause of the crash was *"Improper planning/decision by the pilot, the pilot's failure to maintain proper altitude and clearance over mountainous terrain, and* the copilot's failure to adequately monitor the progress of the flight. Factors related to the accident were: insufficient terrain information provided by the flight service specialist during the preflight briefing after the pilot inquired about a low altitude departure, darkness, mountainous terrain, both pilots lack of familiarity with the geographical area, and the copilot's lack of familiarity with the aircraft."

Dean Paul "Dino" Martin
Dino, Desi and Billy

Died: March 21, 1987, Mount San Gorgonio, Calif.

IN THE 1960S, TWO OF HOLLYWOOD'S "SECOND GENERATION" formed a singing group and joined the "mod generation." Dean Paul "Dino" Martin was the son of singer/actor Dean Martin. Dino's friend, Desi Arnaz, Jr., was the son of television stars Desi Arnaz and Lucille Ball. They recruited their friend Billy Hinshe and formed Dino, Desi and Billy. They enjoyed one major hit, *I'm a Fool*.

After the band split up, Dino tried acting. He was well-received in his performance in the movie *Players*. But his movie career floundered and he took up professional tennis. By 1987, he had also become a captain in the California Air National Guard.

AT 1:55 P.M. MARCH 21, 1987, Dino is at the controls of his F-4C Phantom fighter jet on the runway at March Air Force Base in Riverside County, California. As he takes off, he points the jet almost straight up in a high-speed maximum performance climb. After entering the clouds, the air traffic controller radios instructions to Dino to turn left to avoid an upcoming mountain, but gets no response. Minutes later the jet disappears from the controller's radar screen.

Four days later the wreckage of Dino's jet is discovered near the summit of Mount San Gorgonio. He had struck the granite face of the mountain inverted at nearly 560 miles an hour, instantly killing himself and weapons officer, Capt. Ramon Ortiz.

Investigators believe the G-force of the maximum performance climb and the blinding clouds combined to disorient Dino so that he simply was unable to figure out his airplane's position relative to the mountain.

Kyo Sakamoto
Singer

Died: Aug. 12, 1985, near Tokyo

KYU SAKAMOTO WAS BORN NOV. 10, 1941, in Kawasaki City, Kanagawa Perfecture. At the age of 20, he released *Ue o Muite Aruko (I Look Up When I Walk.)* It was a big enough hit in Japan that two years later it was released in the United States. The U.S. version was retitled, *Sukiyaki.* The new title had no relationship to the song itself. It was simply a Japanese word record executives thought American disc jockeys could pronounce.

In mid-June 1963, *Sukiyaki* became the No. 1 song in America and stayed there for three weeks – the first foreign language song to reach No. 1 in America. He continued to record in Japan where he scored hits with *Shiawase Nara Te o Tatako* and *Miagete Goran Sora no Hoshi o.*

ON AUG. 12, 1985, Kyu boards a JAL 747 for a short flight from Tokyo to Osaka. About 12 minutes into the flight, the passengers feel a strong vibration followed by a loud noise. It is an aft bulkhead failing. Suddenly, an explosive loss of pressure tears off ceiling tiles and blows anything not strapped down out the rear of the plane.

The rupturing bulkhead severs all four of the airplane's hydraulic systems and tears off a 15-foot section of the vertical stabilizer and other parts of the tail section.

The nose of the plane rises quickly and the crew has trouble controlling the airplane. Within a couple of minutes, all of the flight control surfaces – ailerons, elevator and rudder – are uncontrollable and the pilots fight to fly the plane by using the engine thrust. They keep it in the air for more than 30 minutes – long enough for some passengers to write "good-bye" notes to loved ones. But the plane is descending and there is no way to stop it.

First, it strikes trees at the top of a ridge and then slams into Mount Osutaka and disintegrates. Five hundred and twenty of the 524 people on board die instantly, including Kyu. It remains the worse single aircraft accident in history.

Stan Rogers
Folk Singer

Died: June 2, 1989, near Covington, Ky.

STAN ROGERS WAS A BIG MAN WITH A RUMBLING BARITONE, balding head and beard. With a sack full of songs about fishermen and farmers, mariners and miners, he was Canada's champion of the common man, much as Woody Guthrie had been in America.

He abandoned his early career as a Rock 'n Roll bassist in favor of acoustic Folk music. With his first album, *Fogarty's Cove*, he gave voice to the uniquely Canadian experience of life in the Maritimes. He continued paying homage to everyday Canadians with his subsequent albums: *Turnaround; Between the Breaks ... Live; Northwest Passage; For the Family* and *From Fresh Water*.

ON JUNE 2, 1989, Stan is headed home from the Kerrville Folk Festival in Kerrville, Texas, aboard Air Canada Flight 797 - a DC-9, when three circuit breakers trip in the cockpit, indicating a problem with the lavatory flush motors. Smoke begins to come from the lavatory in the rear of the airplane. A flight attendant sprays the lavatory with a fire extinguisher, but black smoke continues to billow from inside the walls.

Moments later, when the airplane develops electrical problems, the pilot declares an emergency and begins to descend toward the Cincinnati/Northern Kentucky International Airport in Covington, Ky.

Despite smoke rapidly filling the cabin, the crew is able safely to make an emergency landing. As soon as the airplane rolls to a stop, the passengers begin to evacuate through the exits. However, the open doors allow fresh air to hit the flames and a "flash fire" erupts throughout the cabin. Twenty-three of the passengers can not get out in time. Among them, Canada's voice of the common man, Stan Rogers.

The NTSB reported that its investigation revealed *"three flush motor circuit breakers had popped about 11 minutes before smoke was detected. The captain misconstrued reports that the fire was abating when he received conflicting fire progress reports. Subsequently, he landed at the Cincinnati International Airport rather than at Louisville, which would have allowed him to land 3 to 5 minutes sooner. Wet towels and breathing through clothes aided survival. Fire source: unknown. Probable cause: miscellaneous equipment/furnishings, lavatories – Fire. Safety advisory: conflicting – other crewmember. Unsafe/hazardous condition: not understood – Pilot in Command."*

Keith Green
Christian Singer

Died: July 28, 1982, Lindale, Texas

BORN IN 1953, KEITH GREEN BECAME A RISING STAR when he was only a child. At the age of 11, he wrote and recorded *The Way I Used to Be,* becoming the youngest member of the American Society of Composers, Authors and Publishers. Within a few years, he had a recording contract with Decca, the same record company that recorded Patsy Cline and Rick Nelson. It was the era of the Teen Idol, and Decca planned for Keith, the "prepubescent dreamboat" as *Time* magazine called him, to be next.

Then Keith's life took an ominous turn. He became involved in drugs, then accepted and abandoned a succession of religions. Finally, in the early 1970s, Keith committed his life to both Christianity and his wife, Melody. With his conversion, Keith began writing and playing Christian/Rock music and quickly became one of the more popular performers of the genre.

His song *You're Love Broke Through* became a staple of performers on Christian concert tours.

Keith and his wife organized an outreach program for those

at the bottom of society – drug addicts, prostitutes, the homeless. Eventually, they moved the entire operation to Lindale, Texas, and named their effort the Last Days Ministries.

Though his records and concerts were immensely popular, Keith – true to his slogan, "No Compromise" – annoyed record companies and concert promoters by refusing to charge for his music. Of the 200,000 copies of his album *So You Wanna Go Back to Egypt*, 60,000 were given away.

Still, the Last Days Ministries was profitable enough to afford leasing a twin-engine Cessna 414 and building a private airstrip on the Ministry's property in Lindale.

ON JULY 28, 1982, Keith puts two of his children, 3-year-old Josiah and 2-year-old Bethany, in the airplane, along with his friends John and Dede Smalley and their six children. He asks pilot Don Burmeister to give them a sightseeing tour of the Last Days Ministries property.

According to the NTSB, "*Witnesses stated that the aircraft departed runway 33 and appeared to over rotate at lift off. The aircraft was observed to climb to about 75 to 100 feet above ground level, then began to sink until it disappeared behind some trees.*"

As it crashes through the trees, the wingtip fuel tanks rupture and spew a fine mist of volatile aviation fuel into the air. Within seconds, it ignites. Everyone on board survives the impact, only to die from smoke inhalation and burns.

The NTSB determined the airplane was 445 pounds overweight and, perhaps worse, the weight was distributed in such as fashion as to make the airplane "tail heavy." Weight and balance computations are the responsibility of the pilot and the NTSB noted that "*59 of his 62 hours (of) multi-engine (time) were as copilot. He had no formal C -414 training and had recorded only*

2 hours of instruction in conventional multi-engine aircraft. He had never been required to perform weight/balance computations in his military flying or any FAA exam or checkrides. Company management did not comply with insurance stipulations which required (the) pilot of the flight to attend a Cessna flight training school, nor did the pilot satisfy the minimum hour requirements."

At the time of the crash, wife Melody was home with their one-year-old daughter Rebekah. She was also six weeks pregnant with their fourth child, Rachel. Today Melody lives in Oceanside, Calif., and continues to work with Last Days Ministries.

John Felton
The Diamonds, Singer

Died: May 17, 1982, outside of Mount Shasta

THE DIAMONDS BECAME A POPULAR "DOO WOP" GROUP of the mid-fifties by recording songs that were already established hits for other acts, including *Why Do Fools Fall in Love* - Frankie Lymon; *Church Bells May Ring* – The Willows; *Little Girl of Mine* – The Cleftones; *KA Ding Dong* – The G Clefs; *Soft Summer Breeze* – Eddie Heywood; and *A Thousand Miles Away* – The Heartbeats.

In February 1957, they had their biggest hit with a remake of The Gladiolas rumba rocker, *Little Darlin'*.

The group went through several personnel changes, with John joining in 1959. His deep booming voice can be heard on the Diamond's 1959 hit, *She Say (Oom dooby doom)* and, also singing the repetitive bass chant on *Alligator*. The Diamonds continued to record into the sixties, but musical tastes were changing and Doo Wop vocal groups found the going harder and harder. The Diamonds managed one more hit, *One Summer Night,* before Mercury Records finally released them from their contract.

On May 17,1982, John, his wife, Linda, and pilot Daniel Jackson, along with his wife, Peggy, climb aboard a single-engine Beech A24R, commonly called a Beech Sierra.

According to the NTSB, the aircraft was en route from Reno, Nev. to Grants Pass, Ore. *"Upon being told by Red Bluff, California Flight Service Station in an in-flight weather briefing that the passes were closed and VFR flight was not recommended, the aircraft landed at Redding, California. After another briefing, the pilot filed a VFR flight plan at 12:13 PDT which was activated at 12:45PDT. The pilot was told three times that VFR flight was not recommended. He told flight service that there was an entertainer aboard who was anxious to get home and that if he encountered any problems with the weather he would head west."*

The airplane crashes on down-sloping terrain about 12 miles northeast of Mount Shasta, apparently in clouds, rain, ice and turbulence. Contributing factors, according to the NTSB, included clouds, turbulence, low ceiling, icing conditions, pressure induced by the pilot in command, lack of total instrument time by the pilot in command, mountainous and hilly terrain, high terrain and trees.

Randy Rhoads
Guitarist, Ozzy Osbourne; Quiet Riot

Died: March 19, 1982, Leesburg, Fla.

RANDALL WILLIAM RHOADS LEARNED TO PLAY on an acoustic Gibson guitar that had been handed down through several generations. He was only six years old when it was given to him. He took lessons at a North Hollywood music school owned by his mother. In his early teens, he grew interested in the electric guitar and saw his musical future while attending an Alice Cooper concert.

By his late teens, Randy had formed the Los Angeles-based band Little Women. They would later become known as Quiet Riot.

Quiet Riot quickly became one of the hotter bands in Los Angeles, and lead guitar player Randy developed a reputation to rival that of Eddie Van Halen. CBS/Japan released two Quiet Riot albums in Japan, which built a large following there and in Europe. However, the band never enjoyed the same level of success in the United States.

Frustrated, Randy auditioned for a new band being assembled by former Black Sabbath front man Ozzy Osbourne. At the audition, Osbourne hired Randy after listening to him play only a few warm up scales.

They went to England and recorded Ozzy's wildly popular solo album, *Blizzard of Ozz*. On the road to promote the album, Randy spectacular guitar work earned him a following of his own.

Quickly after recording *Blizzard of Ozz*, Randy and Ozzy went back in the studio to record *Diary of a Madman*. Before it was mixed, they were back out on the road.

ON MARCH 19, 1982, while on tour promoting the new album, the Ozzy Osbourne show stops in Orlando, Fla. They are to take part in the "Rock Super Bowl XIV" along with several other major acts. Bus driver Andrew Aycock parks the tour bus near his home in neighboring Leesburg, Fla. There is a small airport nearby and Aycock, a pilot, invites several members of the Ozzy entourage to go for a flight.

Randy and makeup artist Rachel Youngblood watch the first group climb into a V35 Bonanza (which Aycock had apparently never been given permission to fly), take off and buzz the neighborhood, making several low altitude passes.

When the first group's ride is over, it is Randy and Rachel's turn.

Again, Aycock makes several low passes over the tour bus and a nearby home, at times dropping below tree level. On the final pass, the airplane's left wing slams into the tour bus and tears off. The fuselage cuts a tree by the sidewalk in half, then slams into a nearby house.

Ozzy awakes inside the bus and hurries out to discover the house engulfed in flames and a gaping hole in the garage. Inside are the remains of his driver, makeup artist and "musical soul mate" Randy.

The NTSB determined the probable cause of the accident was poor judgment by the pilot, buzzing performed by the pilot and misjudged clearance on the part of the pilot.

Jud Strunk
Singer/Songwriter/Comedian

Died: Oct. 5, 1981, Carrabassett, Maine

JUSTIN "JUD" STRUNK WAS BORN IN JAMESTOWN, N.Y., in 1936, but spent most of his life in Farmington, Maine. He began his career in music playing at local clubs, then moved up to the U.S. Armed Forces circuit and finally appeared in an Off-Broadway musical, *Beautiful Dreamer*. After signing with MGM Records, he released *Daisy a Day*. It was his first and biggest hit.

Daisy a Day rose to No. 15 on the Pop charts and made it into the Top 40 on the Country chart. He was as at home on television as on the radio and became a regular performer on *Rowan & Martin's Laugh-In*. He also made multiple appearances on *The Glen Campbell Goodtime Hour* and *Bewitched*. Although he released a number of other singles – *My Country, Next Door Neighbor's Kid* and *The Biggest Parakeets in Town* – none matched the success of *Daisy a Day*.

OCT. 5, 1981 is a beautiful fall day in Carrabassett, Maine – clear skies, light wind, and 20 miles visibility. The kind of day pilots find irresistible. Jud and Carrabassett mayor Dick Ayotte arrive at the airport to take a short sightseeing trip in Jud's open cockpit World War II training airplane, a Fairchild M-62A.

During the takeoff, everything seems normal until the airplane gets about 400 feet in the air. Witnesses notice the nose is pitched up in climbing attitude, but the plane seems not to climb. It turns left for a moment then turns left again and begins to descend. The descent continues and the airplane crashes into a wooded area. Both Jud and Dick are killed instantly.

The NTSB learned Jud had deployed the aircraft's flaps upon take-off, but determined that was only a factor in the accident. Perhaps more to the point, an autopsy revealed Jud had died from coronary thrombosis – a heart attack.

Consequently, the NTSB ruled the probable cause of the accident was incapacitation of the pilot in command due to heart attack. Other factors included the misuse or failure to use flaps.

Bill Chase
Jazz Trumpet

Died: Aug. 9, 1974, Jackson, Minn.

WILLIAM EDWARD CHIAIESE WAS BORN OCT. 20, 1934, in Squantum, Mass. Although he became one of the top trumpeters in the world, early in life he was drummer. He did not begin playing trumpet until his junior year of high school.

He began his collegiate studies at the New England Conservatory, but finished his degree at the Berkeley School of Music in Boston. After graduating, he played with a who's who of top instrumentalists, including Maynard Ferguson, Stan Kenton and Woody Herman.

By the mid-1960s, Chiaiese, who changed his name to the more easily pronounced "Chase," became interested in fusing the jazz to which he was accustomed with the Rock 'n Roll that was dominating the air-waves. He assembled a band that included a searing horn section, a rhythm section and a singer.

He called it Chase. In 1971, Bill was nominated for a Grammy as Best New Artist and shot to national attention with the hit, *Get It On.*

ON AUG. 9, 1974, Bill and his band have just finished playing a series of concerts in Texas and board a small twin-engine, PA-30 Twin Comanche to fly to their next date in Jackson, Minn.

The weather in Jackson is particularly nasty – low clouds, rain and turbulent winds. While attempting to land, the pilot apparently allows the airplane to slow to such a low airspeed that the wings simply quit producing lift and the plane falls from the sky. The wreckage is discovered three-eights of a mile northeast of the airport. Everyone on board is killed, including Bill, his pilot and three members of his band.

The NTSB determined the probable causes of the accident all were the pilot's fault, including failure to obtain and maintain flying speed, improper IFR operation and inadequate preflight preparation and planning.

"Gentleman" Jim Reeves
Singer

Died: July 31, 1964, Nashville, Tenn.

JIM REEVES APPEARED TO BE one of those rare singers with the Midas Touch. However, the string of hits he released in the 1950s and early 1960s was not the result of fate or luck, but the efforts of a hard-working perfectionist.

Born into near poverty in Galloway, Texas, Jim grew up listening to the recordings of Jimmie Rodgers and the Carter Family. He became the star of the Carthage, Texas, high school baseball team and signed a minor league contract with the St. Louis Cardinals after graduating, but an injury forced him out of baseball and into his other love – music.

His smooth baritone voice helped him land a job as an announcer for KWKH radio station in Shreveport, La., the home of the Louisiana Hayride. When Hank Williams failed to show up for a performance in 1952, Jim was allowed to fill in.

It led to a recording contract with a small label for which he produced a big hit, *Mexican Joe*. It went straight to No. 1 on the Country charts. The former baseball player had hit a grand-slam on his first time at bat.

On the strength of *Mexican Joe,* Jim became a regular feature on the Louisiana Hayride. In 1953, he was invited to join the Grand Ole' Opry and signed a contract with RCA Records, too.

Working with legendary producers Chet Atkins and Steve Sholes at RCA, Jim produced an impressive list of hits: *Yonder Comes Sucker, According to My Heart, Four Walls, Blue Boy, Billy Bayou, Am I Losing You, He'll Have to Go* and *Welcome to My World.*

Jim pushed Country music away from its fiddle and steel guitar backwoods sound toward a more Pop-flavored, "cosmopolitan" sound. It was not favored by some Country music traditionalists, but he won converts through network TV appearances, his own ABC network radio program and live performances. World Tours made him an international star, as popular in Asia, Australia, Europe and India as in the United States.

On July 31, 1964, Jim has taken a break from touring and flies in his own single-engine Beechcraft B-33, "Debonair," to Arkansas where he is involved in a business deal concerning some property.

During the return flight with his manager and piano player, Dean Manuel, Jim reports encountering heavy rain over the hills near Nashville. At 4:48 p.m., as Jim is making his approach to the airport, the airplane disappears from the radar screen.

For the next two days, more than 400 people, 12 airplanes and two helicopters search for Jim and his passenger. They eventually find the demolished airplane in a heavily wooded area a few miles from Nashville's Berry Airport. Jim and his passenger had been killed instantly.

Investigators determined the cause of the crash was a common one – Jim had flown his airplane from good weather into bad weather – particularly bad weather.

The NTSB noted that Jim had flown his small airplane in the vicinity of thunderstorms.

With their violent wind shears, a thunderstorm can tear an airplane apart in midair – its micro-bursts can as easily slam it into the ground. Add to that a thunderstorm's blinding rain and damaging hail and it becomes one of the places most pilots assiduously avoid.

For reasons that might never be known, Jim apparently did not avoid the bad weather July 31, 1964, and joined a distressingly long list of other pilots who also flew into bad weather and did not live to explain why.

Harold "David" Box
Singer

Died: Oct. 23, 1964, near Lubbock, Texas

THERE IS PERHAPS NO GREATER IRONY in the world of popular music than the fate of David Box. He was born in Sulphur Springs, Texas, on Aug. 11, 1943, but his family moved a short time later to Lubbock. David grew up in a musical household. His father had ambitions of being a professional Western Swing Fiddler and bought David a guitar for his 8th birthday.

By his teens, David had become such a fan of hometown star Buddy Holly that he put together a sound-a-like band called The Ravens. They performed in the Lubbock area and even made a few recordings at a local studio.

After the death of Buddy Holly, one of those recordings was sent to Cricket Jerry Allison and David was hired to be the new Crickets singer. Coral Records recorded and released the Crickets', *Peggy Sue Got Married* with David singing lead in place of his deceased musical inspiration, Buddy Holly.

David spent the next few years alternating between his studies at the School of American Art in Westport, Conn., where he studied under Norman Rockwell, and recording and performing as a solo act. In 1964, he left school to devote himself to touring and recording in Nashville under the tutelage of Roy Orbison.

At the time, one of his songs, *Little Lonely Summer Girl*, while not a hit nationally, was doing well in the Houston, Texas, area, so David flew there to help promote the record with a few gigs.

WHILE IN HOUSTON, he works with a local band called Buddy and the Kings whose 19-year-old drummer is also a newly licensed pilot.

After a performance in Harris County, Texas, David and his band are flying home to Lubbock in a Cessna 172 when the airplane crashes killing all aboard. Investigators were never able to determine why.

David Box had followed his boyhood dream of being like Holly to an identical and tragic conclusion.

Buddy Holly's parents were the first to pay their respects to David's family. Mr. Holley has been quoted as telling David's father, "It's better you should know this now; people will tell you that time heals the pain, but it doesn't."

INDEX